Contents

COVER
Fun and Easy
MACHINEWORK
AND QUILTWORK
Basic Techniques
for Beginners

D1066590

⬤REFERENCES
● Quilters News Lèttar Magajine (Leman Publication)
● American Quilter (The American Quilters Society)
● Heirloon Machine Quilting (Harriet Hargrave)
● Mastering Machine Applique (Harriet Hargrave)
● Easy Machine Paper Piecing (Carol Doak)
● Feather weight 221 the perfect portable (Nancy Johnson Srebro)
● The Seminole Patchwork (Chery greider Bradkin)
● Spiral Patchwork (Jane Hill)
● Lessons in Machine Piecing (Marsha McCloskey)
● Home Sewing Book (Japan Readers Digest)

★Copyright Ⓒ 1996 YASUKO KURAISHI & ONDORISHA PUBLISHERS., LTD. All rights reserved.
★Published by ONDORISHA PUBLISHERS., LTD.,
11-11 NISHIGOKEN-CHO, SHINJUKU-KU, TOKYO 162, JAPAN.
★Sole Overseas Distributor:Japan Publications Trading CO Ltd.
P. O. Box 5030 Tokyo International, Tokyo, Japan.
★Distributed
・in United States by Kodansha America. INC.
114 Fifth Avenue, New York, NY 10011, U.S.A
・in British Isles & European Continent by Primier Book MarketING LTD.,
1 GOwer Street, London WCIE 6HA , England.
・in Australia by Bookwise International.
54 Crittenden Road, Findon, South Australia 5023, Australia.
10 9 8 7 6 5 4 3 2 1
ISBN 0-87040-981-6
Printed in Singapore

PATCHWORK QUILTS TO BRIGHTEN YOUR LIFE

By harmonizing cloth, cotton, and human hands you can make eternal designs. However, for these designs to be eternal, you must always bear in mind their usefulness in daily life. It is easier to use casual quilting in daily life than to wear yourself out making complicated designs. One design method is to omit the extra color and effort, so that as the creations are used and washed, they become part of the quilting used in your everyday life.

WEARABLE PATCHWORK

This is quilting you can wear. Quilting is usually flat but this process puts the techniques and designs to use in clothes. America mainly uses pattern sewing. First, prepare the pattern you like and think about how you can incorporate it into your creation. As you learn the various techniques, you'll enjoy machinework and quilting more and more!

CREATING DESIGNS BY SEWING MACHINE

Whether sewn by hand or machine, not all of these designs will suit all clothes. When doing quiltwork by sewing machine, consider the design and technique. It is better to add machinework according to how the creation will be used. Especially by sewing machine you can make practical creations, but it is important that the creation be stylish and easy to use. Designing is not only the use of color and effort; sometimes it is important to omit these in making quilts for everyday use.

USING MACHINES FOR QUILTWORK

The sewing machine was developed to sew quickly and evenly. Of course these are important elements in making patchwork quilts with a sewing machine, but sewing and cutting are also completely different from quilting by hand. It is important to find new designs that can be used in machinework quilting. Traditional patterns join triangles and squares to make units.

※Units are combinations of small shapes that can be joined into blocks.

TYPES OF MATERIALS

Cotton is typically used in quilting, but depending on the creation, ribbons, lace, or Tyrolean tape can be used. Especially when sewing different types of cloth, it is better to join them by machine. When using old silk, attach it to adhesive cloth. When using cotton cloth, spray it with water to prepare it.

TOOLS NEEDED FOR QUILTWORK

①Rotary Cutter
②Mat
③Ruler
(easier to use if non-slip pads are attached)
④Freezer Paper
⑤Adhesive Cloth
⑥Safety Pins
⑦Stick-type Glue
⑧Water Spray Bottle
⑨Ripper
⑩Punch
⑪French Chalk
⑫Sandpaper
⑬Double-sided Tape
⑭Walking Foot
⑮Darning Foot (Quilting Foot)
　other sewing tools

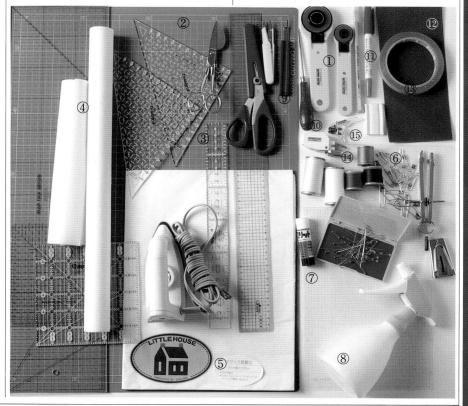

BEFORE THE LESSON

About the Sewing Machine

Description of Each Part

①Presser Foot
②Tension Block
③Stitch Width Regulator
④Sewing Spool
⑤Bobbin Winder
⑥Stitch Length Regulator
⑦Bobbin, Bobbin Case

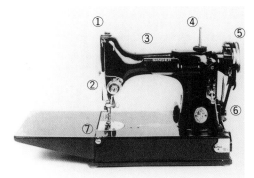

Threading the Upper Thread

This depends on the machine used. The diagram shows a generalized machine. The needle may be threaded from the left, right, or front side.

Bobbin and Bobbin Case

①When thread is wound onto the bobbin, put it into the bobbin case. Whether the end of the thread goes up or down depends on the machine.

②Insert thread into the bobbin case.

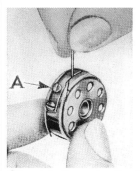

③Insert farther and pull out.

Pulling out the Lower Thread by the Top Thread

①After threading the upper needle, lower the needle and pull out the bottom thread.

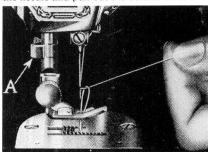

②Pull the top and bottom threads away toward the opposite side. Always try to

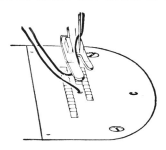

Regulating the Stitch Length

Regulate this by using the Stitch Length Regulator to find the appropriate stitch length.

Taking Care of Your Sewing Machine

Daily care is important in maintaining your sewing machine. Always try to keep the hook free of lint and dust, especially after quilting. Positions for oiling depend on the machine. Refer to the instruction manual and put one or two drops on. After this, try to sew until the oil is gone. If you use your machine every day, oil your machine once a week. Some machines make noise when they need oiling.

About the Tension Block

Tension is the tightness of the top and bottom threads. In order to sew beautifully, keep an even balance between the top and bottom threads. Upper thread tension increases with higher dial numbers.

①Well-Balanced Stitches

②Poorly-Balanced Stitches. Upper thread is too tight.

③Poorly-Balanced Stitches. Lower thread is too tight.

Relationship of Sewing Machine Needles, Thread, and Cloth

Needle / Thread	9 (70)	11, 12 (80)	11, 12 (90)	(110)	14 (110, 120)
Fine Embroidery Thread(60)	○	○			
Embroidery Thread(30) Nylon Thread		○			
Cotton Thread (30 - 60) Nylon Thread		○	○	○	
Polyester Thread		○	○	○	
Polyester-Coated Cotton Thread			○		
Buttonhole Thread Denim Thread					○
Fabric	Josette	Cotton	Cotton	Knit	Jeans
Use		Quilting Most Common Needle			

※needle gauge increases with thickness
※thread gauge increases with fineness of thread
( ) indicates Western needle gauges

[1] Holding the Rotary Cutter

Hold the rotary cutter as you would a knife. Holding the left side of the blade to the ruler, keep steady pressure on the cutter till the end is reached.

[2] Using the Rotary Cutter

①Try to use the full width of the cloth by cutting a 110 cm (43") strip. Try to match up the selvages.

②The upper side is the selvage, the lower side is rounded. Place the ruler under the fold and place another ruler perpendicular to the first one.

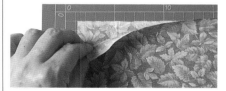

③Cut off the edge.

④The edge is now straight. The photo shows a cloth folded into quarters and cut.

⑤Cut to the necessary width. Keep in mind that the seam on both sides is 1.5 cm (5/8").

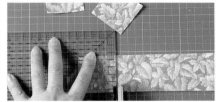

⑥Cut off a strip with a seam whenever it is called for. Eight strips may be placed upon each other and cut at the same time.

[3] Checking Seams

When machine piecing, determine the seam based on the presser foot. The width of the presser foot depends on the machine used. Try to sew several strips to find out the best position for your presser foot to make a 0.7 cm (1/4") seam.

[4] Straight Piecing

①Match the edge of the cloth to the right edge of the presser foot. Pull the top and bottom threads in opposite directions.

②Continue sewing straight. The allowance will be between the right edge of the presser foot and the position of the lowered the needle. If a 0.7 cm (1/4") allowance cannot be made with the presser foot, try placing tape onto the needle plate.

[5] Chain Piecing

①Place two pieces of cloth front to front and begin sewing.

②Continue sewing the second unit without cutting the thread.

③Keep on sewing pieces one after the other. This is called "Chain Piecing".

④Cut the pieces one by one from the chain.

[6] Ironing

①Fold seam down and iron

②Open seam and iron. Whether the seam is opened or folded depends on what is most suitable.

TERMS USED IN MACHINE QUILTING
Sewing Machine Terms, Quilting Terms

TOOLS

Rotary Cutter
The blade is round. Roll blade along edge of ruler placed on cloth.

Cutting Mat
Always place this under the cloth when using the rotary cutter.

Walking Foot
This attachment allows smooth sewing of rough cloth. Use this for quilting straight lines.

Quilting Foot (Darning Foot)
Use this for embroidering or to join pieces together in Free Motion Quilting. Move the needle; do not change direction of cloth when using this foot.

MATERIALS

Backing
Cloth that is placed with cotton in quilting. Quilt through this cotton and thread. Quilting can be stopped here, or lining can also be added.

Batting
Quilt cotton

Nylon Thread
Clear thread for blind stitch applique or quilting.

Adhesive Cloth
Cloth with adhesive on one or both sides (paper cloth).

Freezer Paper
One side has plastic that becomes sticky when ironed. This is often used to make shapes for applique and machine quilting.

METHODS

Sewing Line
When the stitch width is set at zero, you can sew straight. The place where the needle contacts the cloth is called the sewing line. Move this to the left and right when sewing zigzags.

Stitch Width
The width moved to the right and left when sewing a zigzag. If this is made smaller, it becomes a satin stitch.

Stitch Length
Distance between consecutive stitches. Length of stitches.

Pressed Quilt
Method where the cloth is placed on the backing cloth and quilt cotton, and sewn together. Quilting can be done simultaneously.

Chain Piecing
Method of piecing by sewing continuously without cutting the thread. Very efficient and fast. (Refer to page 5)

Piecing
Join pieces together.

Strip Piecing
Method where strips of cloth are joined back to front.

Strip
Cloth cut long and narrow.

String Piecing
Piecing cloth of uneven sizes.

Donut Cut
Rings cut off after piecing. Remove stitches and arrange.

Paper Piecing
Method where the pattern is drawn on paper, the cloth is placed on back, and sewn.

Blind Stitch Applique
Method where stitching is not seen from the front. Use clear thread for machine stitching.

Satin Stitch Applique
Applique using very fine zigzag stitch.

Cutout Applique
Attach adhesive cloth to cloth with large pattern, cut off desired portion of pattern make a new design, and applique. In French this is known as Broderie Perse.

Fabric Manipulation
Changing the appearance of the cloth. Often used for wearable creations.
Folding cloth (Prairie Point)
Shrinking (Gather)
Tying (Tie)
Cutting (Slash)
Pleating (Pleats)

Quilt As You Go
This method allows you to take the quilting with you anywhere. To do this, make small blocks. So make small blocks first and join pieces together later. It is difficult to machine quilt large things, so use Quilt As You Go; make small blocks and join them later.

Drop Field
Lower the feed dog. Sew the drop field by Free Motion.

DESIGN

Seminole (refer to page 54)
After strip piecing, cut off diagonally or straight, offset the seam, and sew together again and make the design. This is a famous design of the Seminole Indians of Florida.

Spiral (refer to page 56)
Piece by offsetting strips to make a twisted tube. Cut this into donut shapes remove the stitches from one side, arrange, and piece together again.

Bajero (refer to page 58)
This pattern is used in Europe for needlepoint on chairs, and has been adapted to quiltwork. One piece is the same as one stitch in needlepoint. Make a tube by strip piecing, and cut this into donut shapes remove the stitches from one side, arrange, and sew together again.

Fracture (refer to page 59)
This means division or dissolution. Consider

balance when cutting cloth with large patterns to obtain the desired effect.

Drop Quilt
A method that uses quilting between pieced sections. Use walking foot.

Outline Quilt
Piece 0.7 cm (1/4") from piecing or applique line.

Echo Quilt
Method of quiling seen in Hawaiian quilts.

Stipple Quilt
(Meander Quilt) Quilt in flowing lines, taking care not to cross quilt lines. Use the darning foot (Quilting Foot)

Continuous Design
When quilting designs by machine, this single-line design is often used because of its convenience.

Surface Design
Surface design made of cloth. This is usually used in wearable creations.

NAMES OF QUILT PARTS

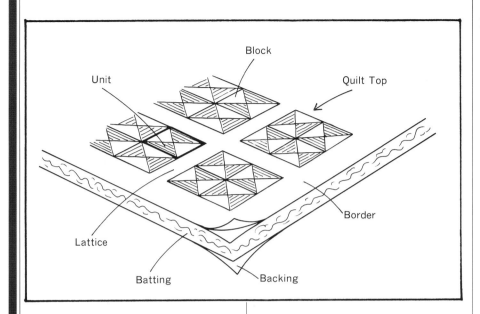

- Unit
- Block
- Quilt Top
- Border
- Lattice
- Batting
- Backing

SET METHOD FOR BLOCKS

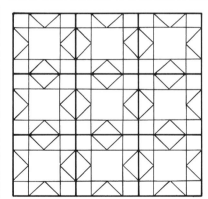

Continuous set

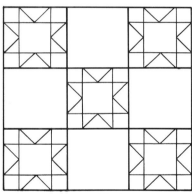

Set offset by one block

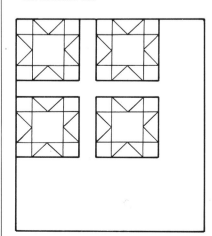

Set with lattice

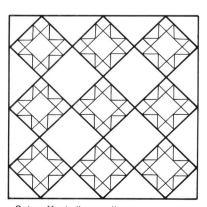

Sets offset diagonally

FINISHING THE EDGES

Attach border cloth (finish border corners at 45° or straight)

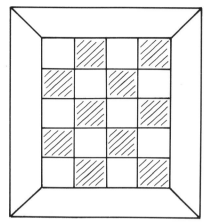

Roll up batting

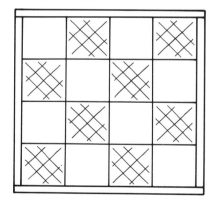

※Refer to Lesson 8; Finishing the Quilt for methods of attaching borders and finishing binding

LESSON 1

JOINING THE SQUARES

[1] SQUARE

①This is a different way of joining squares than just sewing and cutting two strips. It is convenient for using small pieces of cloth or piecing scraps.

②Cut squares in advance. Make a cross in the center of one square and match squares together.

③Line up the center with the edge of the presser foot, sew together 0.7 cm (1/4") on each side of center line.

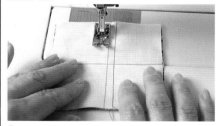

④Cut along the center line

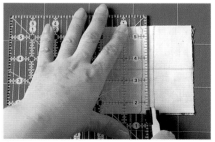

⑤Compare with photo after cutting.

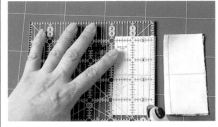

⑥Join two cut cloth squares with different right sides. Extend center lines.

⑦Sew along sides of center line as in the first step.

⑧Cut along the center line.

⑨Completed joining of two sets of squares

⑩Back side.

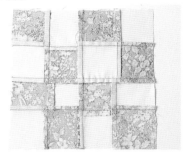

[2] RECTANGLE

①This is another easy way to combine small blocks into a square.

②Match two pieces together precisely the center with the edge of the presser foot.

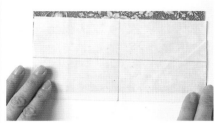

③Sew together 0.7 cm (1/4") on each side of the center line.

④Cut along center line.

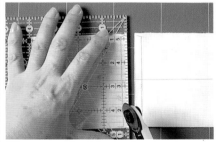

⑤Draw center line following direction of pattern.

⑥Match foot with centerline as in step ②.

⑦Sew along both sides of center line.

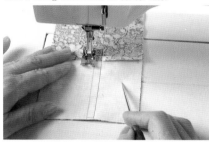

⑧Cut along center line.

⑨Two sets of joined rectangles are completed.

⑩Back side.

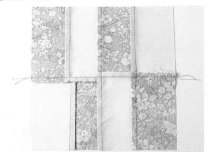

[3] DIAMOND

①This is a joined diamond with a 60° center. Joining six pieces makes a hexagram, and cutting at 45° makes an octagon.

②Spread out the strip-pieced cloth. Place the ruler as shown in the photo to mark at 60°on one side of the cloth.

③Cut.

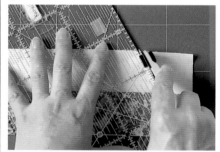

④Rotate the cloth and cut at 60° from the left side. Be sure to cut the same length and width as shown in the photo.

⑤Arrange as in photo.

⑥Sew together two cut pieces. This time, the point of the triangle on the opposite side must stick out 0.7 cm (1/4"), as in the photo. Hold seam matching this.

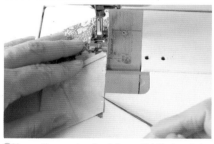

⑦Sew together with a 0.7 cm (1/4") seam.

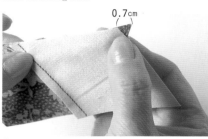

⑧You will see why the 0.7 cm (1/4") tip of the triangle sticks out.

⑨You can sew even joined seams like these beautifully.

⑩Turn inside-out

⑪Back side.

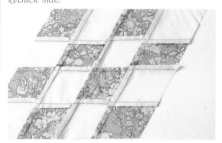

[4] TRAPEZOID

①This is an example of the kind of work done with trapezoids like this. This can be used in hexagon (flower garden) piecing.

②Piece together two strips

③Hold the left side of the cut side and cut again at 60°.

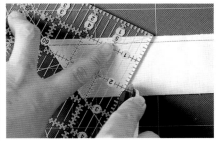

④It should appear as in the photo.

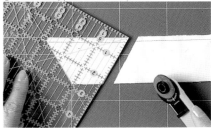

⑤Cut like this.

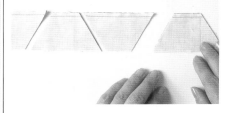

⑥Open the seams and join cloth alternately.

⑦Front side.

⑧Join two pieces together with 0.7 cm (1/4") of triangle protruding.

⑨Line up the presser foot with the edge and sew ahead. When the center of the cloth is reached, the needle should go down and the presser foot should go up.

⑩With the presser foot up, match the top and bottom cloth with a punch and then lower the presser foot. Continue sewing to the protruding corner of the triangle.

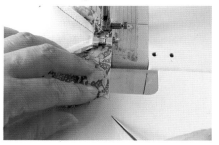

⑪Sewing is completed.

⑫Carefully sew the edge from the front.

⑬Back side of the entire cloth.

LESSON 2

JOINING THE TRIANGLES

[1] SQUARE, ISOSCELES TRIANGLE

①Two right triangles make up the square. Use it for traditional patterns, such as monkey wrench, basket, etc.

②It's okay to draw the square on the cloth, but this time draw it on paper. Draw the square and diagonal line on paper as shown in the photo. The size of the square will depend on the size of the triangle desired. Decide side "a" first using a + 2 cm (3/4") + 0.7 cm (1/4") = x and draw the square with sides of x by x.

③Join the two pieces of cloth together, place the paper with measured squares and diagonals on top, and insert a marking pin.

④Match the edge presser foot with the diagonal line.

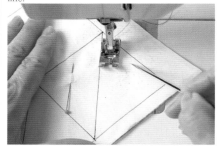

⑤It is important that the diagonal line and presser foot are lined up while sewing.

⑥In the photo sewing begins to the right of the line, the cloth is rotated when the other side is reached, and sewing is continued to the left of the line.

⑦When the edge of the triangle is reached, raise both the needle and presser foot.

⑧Do not sew the corner of the triangle (you can see in the photo where the thread is free). Match the edge of the presser foot with the diagonal of the next triangle and continue sewing.

⑨Sew the opposite side of the diagonal line as shown in the photo.

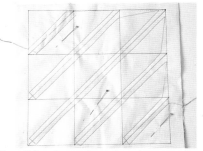

⑩Cut off the edges and cut along the perpendicular lines.

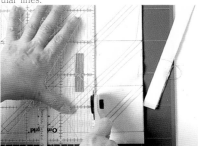

⑪Cut as in the photo.

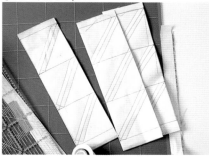

⑫Cut off the square blocks one by one.

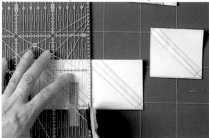

⑬The squares should look like this.

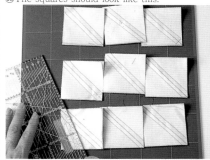

⑭Cut along diagonal lines.

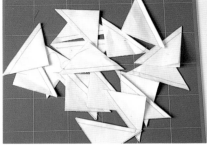

⑮Remove paper by pulling cloth and paper in opposite directions.

⑯Paper along the seam should be removed by pulling sideways.

⑰Turn to the right side and remove the extra seam and triangle points

⑱Completed squares.

⑲Arrange according to the design.

⑳Back side.

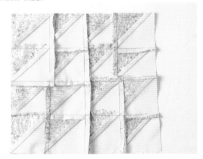

[2] FOUR-TRIANGLE SQUARE

①The square is divided into four triangles along diagonal lines. This triangle joining is used for the broken dish and Ohio Star patterns.

②Draw diagonal lines on one side of two joined pieces of cloth. If the triangles desired are a, a, b, the size of cloth needed is $b = \sqrt{a^2 + a^2} = \sqrt{2a^2}$ Prepare two pieces of cloth measuring b + 4 cm

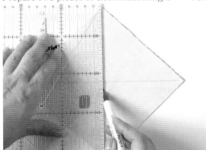

③Joint the squares and sew together) 0.7 cm (1/4") from each side of the diagonal lines.

④Cut along the diagonal after sewing.

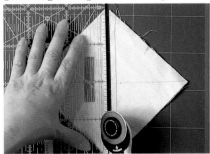

⑤Match the two triangles, alternating the colors.

⑥Draw the diagonal line again for sewing.

⑦As before, sew 0.7 cm (1/4") from each side of the diagonal line.

⑧Cut along the diagonal lines.

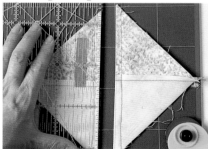

⑨After opening. Two completed sets of matching triangles.

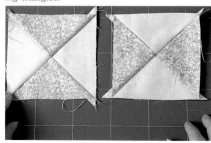

⑩Back side.

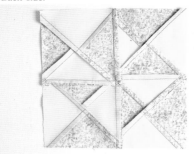

[3] RECTANGLE OF ISOSCELES TRIANGLES

①A right triangle cut along the diagonal of a rectangle. Used for star patterns, trees, etc.

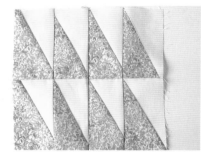

②Two rectangular pieces of cloth (twice as long as wide) and paper for the pattern cut diagonally.

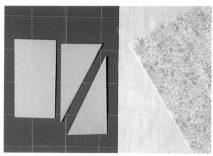

③Match the two pieces of cloth. Place the pattern paper on top, matching the edges, and place the ruler on top. If the cloth has a back and a front, it is important that the fronts of both are on top or the bottom.

④Cut the cloth, taking care not to cut the paper.

⑤Place the other piece of pattern paper on the cloth pointing up.

⑥Remove the ruler and place it on the cloth.

⑦Cut the other cloth in the same way.

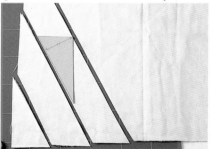

⑧Cut parallel bias strips in the first cloth.

⑨Iron the two cut strips (to prevent moving).

⑩Place the pattern paper and ruler on the strip.

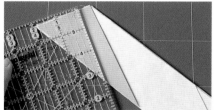

⑪Cut the cloth alternately.

⑫Cutting is completed.

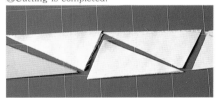

⑬Open them up.

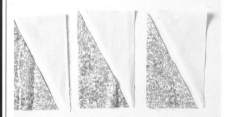

⑭Match the points on alternate pieces of cloth and sew together.

⑮Finished pieces look like this.

⑯Back side.

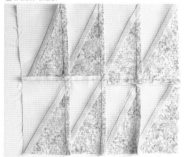

[4] EQUILATERAL TRIANGLE

①Equilateral triangles have 60° angles and three equal sides. These triangles can be used for the thousand pyramid.

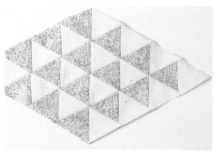

②Sew 0.7 cm (1/4") seam along both sides of two strips.

③Cut at 60° from the edge. Cut the next piece 60° from the other side. It is very important not to interfere with the other seam.

④Cut one after another and open up.

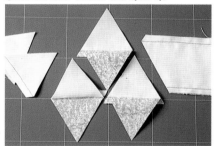

⑤Join two matching pieces and sew. Join four pieces and sew.

⑥Back side.

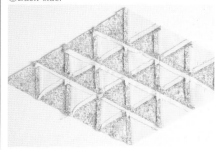

LESSONS 1 AND 2
USEFUL CREATIONS
A HAPPY KITCHEN

Just fresh-baked bread and coffee is enough for a picnic on a warm Spring day.

LESSON 3

LOG CABIN AND PINEAPPLE

[1] LOG CABIN DARK AND LIGHT

①The Log Cabin pattern is very well-suited to machine piecing. The pattern can be made by joining cloth of different colors or patterns.

②Center cloth is 4.5 cm (1 3/4")×4.5 cm (1 3/4"). Pink strip is 4.5 cm (1 3/4") × 110 cm (44"). Blue strip is 4.5 cm (1 3/4") × 110 cm (44").

③Place the center cloth on the pink strip. Sew only the red piece.

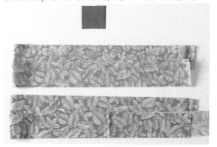

④Cut pink strip to match the red piece and open.

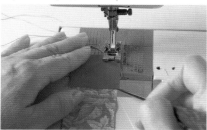

⑤Place the pink strip on the right side of the sewn piece and sew together.

⑥Cut length of pink strip to match.

⑦Open.

⑧Place blue cloth on and sew. Cut length of blue strip to match.

⑨Open.

⑩Back side of finished cloth.

[2] LOG CABIN COURTHOUSE STEPS

①This is different from the Light and dark pattern in that the pieces are joined to the left and right, and top and bottom.

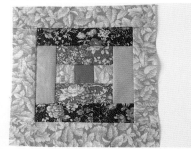

②Sew on pieces of pink cloth the same length as the center piece.

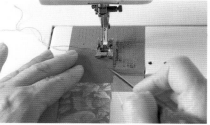

③Sew on the left and right sides and open.

④Sew on the top blue piece.

⑤Sew on the bottom blue piece.

⑥Back side of finished cloth.

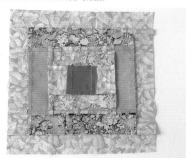

[3] LOG CABIN CHEVRON

①Sew from the piece of cloth that will be at the center

②Sew the pink strip to the corner piece.

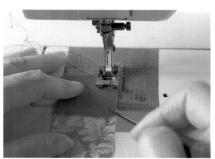

③Cut and open.

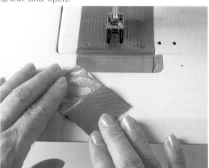

④Sew on the blue strip next.

⑤Cut and open.

⑥Sew pink sections together, then join blue sections.

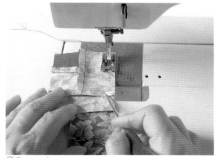

⑦Cut and open.

⑧Back side of finished piece.

PINEAPPLE

①Though this pattern looks hard, the sewing and cutting are the same as in the log cabin pattern, so it's easy!

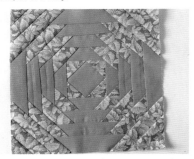

②Center piece is 5.5 cm (2 3/16")×5.5 cm (2 3/16"). Plain strip is 3.5 cm (2 3/8")×110 cm (44"). Printed strip is 3.5 cm (2 3/8")×110 cm (44").

③Sew the first strip to the center piece.

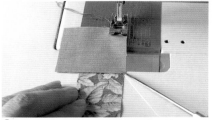

④Sew another strip on the opposite side.

⑤Open.

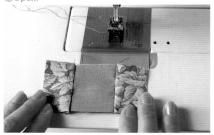

⑥Sew the inside edges of the top and bottom of printed strips.

⑦Sew on four sides and open.

⑧Place the ruler on the cloth so a square edge can be made 0.7 cm (1/4") from the seam.

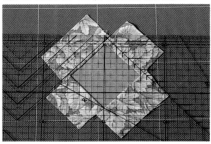

⑨Leave the 0.7 cm (1/4") seam and trim the edges of the printed cloth.

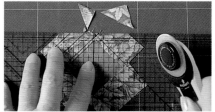

⑩Cut off the border edges.

⑪Sew plain strip on as in photo.

⑫Sew plain strip to next side.

⑬Open. The strips can also be sewn on clockwise.

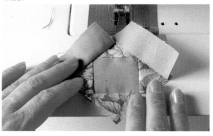

⑭Sew the plain strips to all sides, making sure not to overlap seams.

⑮Trim 0.7 cm (1/4") from seams as before.

⑯Sew printed cloth on next.

⑰Attach next printed cloth.

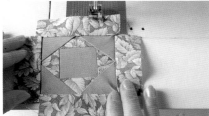

⑱At this step the printed cloth must be cut at the tips of the triangles of plain cloth. Place the ruler parallel to the plain cloth as in the photo.

⑲Join the plain cloth as before. Length of cloth should be the same as the printed cloth.

⑳Attach like this.

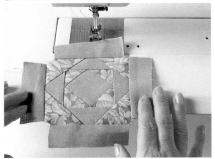

㉑Line up the ruler with the printed cloth in the previous step and cut.

㉒The cloth so far.

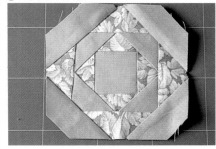

㉓Make a square block and finish. Sew plain cloth to the plain cloth section.

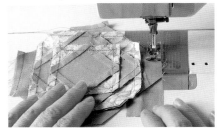

㉔Attach like this.

㉕Cut off extra parts.

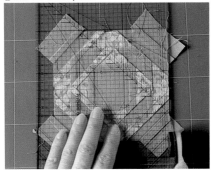

㉖Form a square.

㉗Back side of the large pineapple.

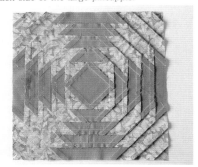

LESSON 3
USEFUL CREATIONS
FOR PEACEFUL SLEEP
The light and dark pattern called log cabin is very popular and is recommended for people wondering about doing machine piecing. Even large projects can be done quickly.

BEDCOVER———Instructions on page 68

LESSON 4
A VARIETY OF STARS

[1] HEXAGRAM

①This hexagram is made by joining diamonds of the same size. Let's try making diamonds from a strip.

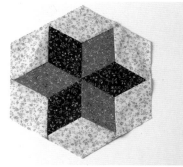

②Prepare three strips of cloth of equal width.

③Place the strips atop each other carefully and iron flat. Cut off at 60° from the right edge.

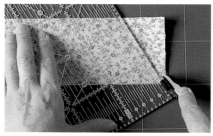

④Turn the cloth so the cut edge is on the left side and cut parallel to the left edge so that the bottom width is the same length as the left edge.

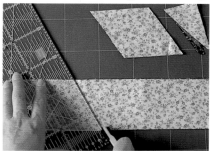

⑤Cut as many pieces as necessary.

⑥Mark on both sides 0.7 cm (1/4") from all four corners .

⑦Sew a seam between the marks.

⑧Open up.

⑨Place white cloth on red cloth and sew between the marks.

⑩Next sew the blue cloth to the white cloth. With the presser foot up and the needle lowered, turn the cloth.

⑪Sew between marks.

⑫Back side of three diamonds sewn together.

⑬Make three identical blocks. Sew the three blocks together. Sew the last white diamonds on as before.

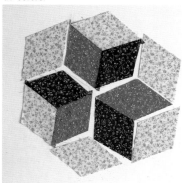

⑭Back side.

Drawing the hexagram.

Draw a circle of the desired size. Divide the circumference of the circle by the radius and make a hexagon by connecting the points. Draw diagonal lines through the center. Mark at points one half of the radius.

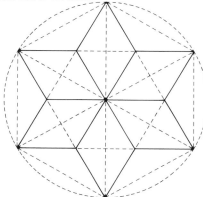

[2] EIGHT-POINTED STAR

①Here is the star. Make your own pattern and begin.

②Prepare necessary cloth for each part.

③Place the pattern and ruler on the cloth and cut. Four to eight layers may be cut this way.

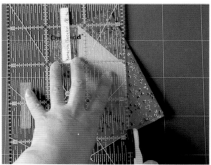

④Cut the number of pieces needed.

⑤Completed cutting of parts.

⑥Refer to the joining of the hexagram (page 24). Join red and blue "A" parts. The key to making the star beautiful is to sew about the length of the tip of the needle from the edge. Join part "C" as well.

⑦Sew two units together. This time, when you start, at the center, place the presser foot about the length of the tip of the needle from the center, and join to the edge cloth gradually.

⑧Join the units as in the photo.

⑨Back view of completed star.

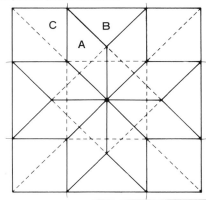

Drawing the eight-pointed star.

Draw a square of the desired size. Make diagonal lines from the corners. Divide the square into sixteenths. Measure lengths from the center of the large square and corners of the small squares equal to the length of the sides of the small squares. Be sure to add 0.7 cm (1/4") to all sides of pattern pieces for seams.

[3] OHIO STAR

①The Ohio star is made by joining nine patches. After joining the triangles into squares, we can make it quickly with the sewing machine.

③Back side

②Instructions for the four-triangle square are in Lesson 2. Let's join the four-triangle square to the squares.

[4] SAWTOOTH STAR

①This is called the sawtooth star because of its jagged edges.

②Try to make a 20 cm (8") block sample. This is made from sixteen 4 cm (1 1/2") dark blue squares, one 11.5 cm 4 1/2") dark blue printed cloth square, four 11.5 cm × 6.5 cm (4 1/2" × 2 1/2") printed white rectangles, eight 6.5 cm (2 1/2") printed red squares, and four 6.5 cm (2 1/2") printed white squares.

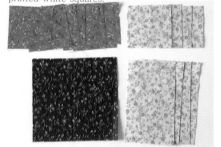

③Draw diagonal lines on all of the red pieces.

④Place 6.5 cm (2 1/2") printed red Squares pieces on both edges of an 11.5 cm × 6.5 cm (4 1/2" × 2 1/2") printed white rectangle.

⑤Match the edges of the red and white cloth and sew along the diagonal line.

⑥Cut 0.7 cm (1/4") from the sewn diagonal line.

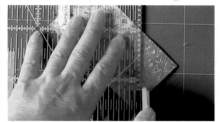

⑦After cutting.

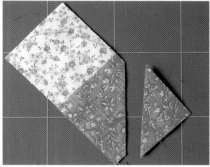

⑧Open the sewn cloth. Place on red cloth for opposite side.

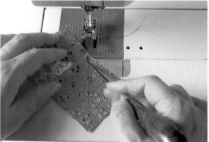

⑨Sew together on diagonal lines.

⑩In the same way, cut off 0.7 cm (1/4") form diagonal lines.

⑪It should look like this.

⑫Sew the nine pieces together as in the photo.

⑬Back side.

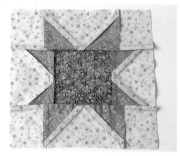

PAGE 29
LESSON 4
USEFUL CREATIONS
LOVELY INTERIORS
Relax comfortably at home with your favorite creations. Even plain living rooms will be revived with these magnificent star variations. It's easy to match colors, too.
CUSHIONS————Instructions on page 68
WALL HANGINGS Instructions on page 69

LESSON 5
APPLIQUE

[1] BLIND STITCH APPLIQUE

①Applique gives the same effect as doing blind stitching by hand with clear thread.

②Tools and Materials; ①freezer paper to copy the patterns, ② cloth for the applique, ③ base cloth for applique, ④ nylon thread, ⑤ spool if thread (100% cotton), ⑥ stick-type glue, ⑦ sprayer.

③Cut out each pattern from the freezer paper and iron them to the back of the cloth.

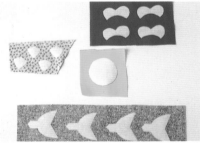

④Cut out each piece leaving 0.5 cm (3/16") for the seam. Apply stick-type glue to seam.

⑤The seam of the circle should be folded after gluing.

⑥Cut off the inner curved portion.

⑦Glue the seam of the petal and fold it carefully with the fingertips.

⑧Fold twice if the pointed part is over 90°. If they are under 90°, fold the tip first, glue both sides, and fold.

⑨Fold the seams except at points of attachment. Place the pattern on the base cloth.

⑩Attach with stick pins pointing towards center as in photo.

⑪Using cotton thread as the bobbin thread and nylon thread as the top thread, sew on with fine zigzag stitch, removing stick pins as you go.

⑫After finishing the center of the flower, sew on petals.

⑬Next, sew on the blossoms.

⑭Completed sewing of the applique.

⑮turn over and remove the inside of the stitching.

⑯Remove the base cloth inside the blossoms and petals.

⑰Spray the back with water.

⑱Remove the freezer paper.

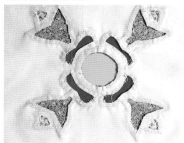

⑲All the freezer paper is removed as in photo. Turn over and iron.

[2] SATIN STITCH APPLIQUE

①The satin stitch is used on cotton for applique used in quilting.

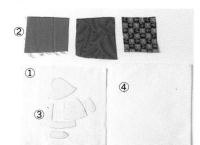

②Materials
① Base Cloth ② Applique Cloth ③ Pattern Paper ④ Double-Sided Adhesive Cloth

③Iron desired cloth onto exposed surface of double-sided tape.

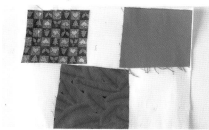

④Place pattern paper onto back of double sided adhesive cloth and copy pattern.

⑤Cut out each piece.

⑥Remove backing from double-sided adhesive cloth, place on base cloth to match pattern, and iron into position.

⑦Place base cloth on cotton (or better yet, stiff polyester), and pin in place.

⑧Applique using satin stitch. Detail of stitching depends on pattern. When sewing applique to cloth, make sure thread goes through edge of pattern piece and cloth. When sewing adjacent pattern pieces, make sure thread goes through both pieces.

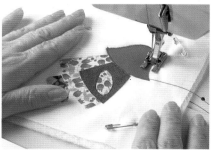

⑨Back side.

[3] CUTOUT APPLIQUE

①This type of applique, known as "Broderie Perse" in French, was widely used in America in the 1700's for making chintz bed covers.

②Apply double-sided adhesive cloth to the back the desired pattern (larger pattern is preferred).

③Remove desired pattern and make a new pattern on base cloth.

④After arranging pieces, remove backing from each piece.

⑤Place pieces on cloth and iron in position.

⑥Stitch edges with satin stitch.

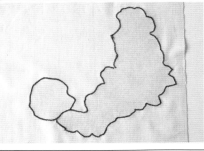

⑦Reverse should look like this.

LESSON 6

EASY STRIP PIECING

(Design 1)

①This very popular pattern, called the "Rail Fence" is made of pieces cut to the same width combined using strip piecing.Changing the color combinations makes it very interesting.

②Cut four strips to the same width.

③Sew together with strip piecing as in the photo.

④Measure width of strip pieced section. Cut sections with the same width.

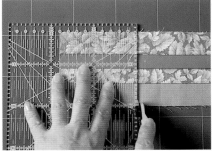

⑤Arrange.

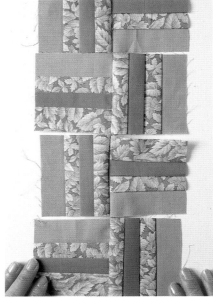

⑥Sew together.

⑦Sewn as a chain.

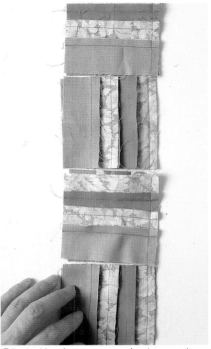

⑧Back side when sewn together into a unit.

(Design 2)

①This square-in-square design is made by cutting strip pieced sections at 45°.

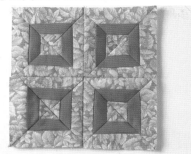

②Cut three strips of the same width.

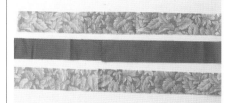

③Sew with a 0.7 cm(1/4") seam.

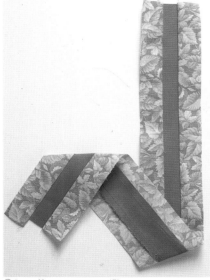

④Cut off one corner at 45°.

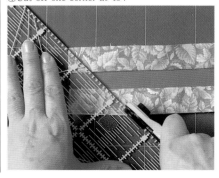

⑤Cut one after another at 45°.

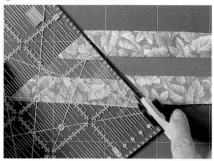

⑥Join two pieces and sew edge to edge.

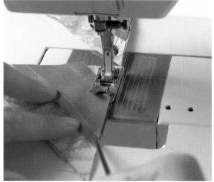

⑦Sew as in photo.

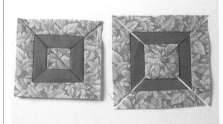

⑧Reverse view of four squares sewn together.

LESSON 5
USEFUL CREATIONS
MERRY CHRISTMAS

A blizzard of presents in Christmas colors. Children will be thrilled to receive these hand-made gifts. Even though it's cold out, inside the air is filled with the warm aroma of Christmas cooking.

WALL HANGING—Instructions on page 70
PICTURE FRAME Instructions on page 70
WREATH (BIG, SMALL)——
                    Instructions on page 71
ORNAMENT (TREE, BOOTS, WALL HANG-
ING)———Instructions on page 71~73

LESSON 6 / USEFUL CREATIONS
BLOWING IN THE WIND, MONOCHROME

Use these extremely functional and stylish bags for picnics on Spring days. They're washable and durable.

TOTE BAG————Instructions on page 74
RUCKSACK————Instructions on page 74

LESSON 7

QUILTING

[1] SHOULD I SEW BY HAND OR MACHINE?

Whether you sew piecework or applique to quilting by hand or machine is entirely up to you. The left photo shows hand stitched quilting, and the right photo shows machine stitched quilting. Hand sewn works look softer, while machine stitching looks sharper. But, when you adapt to machine stitching, you'll come to appreciate the speed and interesting designs that can be created.

[2] MATERIALS AND TOOLS NEEDED FOR MACHINE QUILTING

① Quilting Pencil ② French Chalk (Water-Soluble Ink) ③ Thread (100% Cotton, Nylon) ④ Large and Small Safety Pins (to attach top and bottom liners) ⑤ Thimbles ⑥ Walking Foot, Darning Foot, Quilting Foot ⑦ Cloth (Cotton)

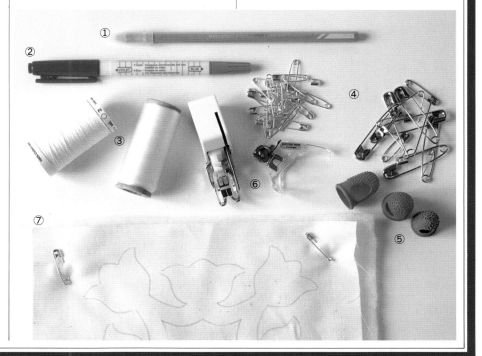

[3] TYPES OF COTTON AND MACHINE QUILTING

Batting comes in three types; 100% cotton, 100% polyester, and mixtures of the two. The thickness of the batting depends on the company that produces it. Choose whichever will best suit your craft.

A 100% Cotton Batting
This expands when used in quilting and contracts when washed.

B 100% Polyester Batting
This is the fluffiest. Even after washing repeatedly it fluffs right up. Needles pass though this easily.

C Combining the natural feeling of cotton and the durability of polyester, this is the material most used in America for bed covers. It gains an antique appearance with use.

A

B

C

[4] TYPES AND METHODS OF QUILTING

A Straight Line

This is the method for quilting checkerboard and diamond patterns.

Quilting stitch size	Machine Stitch
--	2 (too small)
- -	3 (just right)
— — — — — — — — — — —	4 (too large)

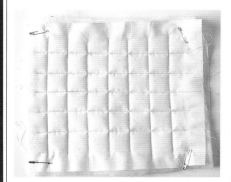

Straight Line

Draw the stitch line on top of the quilting. Attach the cotton and backing cloth with safety pins, and quilt in one direction with walking foot.

Checkerboard

After finishing sewing in one direction, rotate cloth 90° and sew along other stitch lines. Use same method for diamond pattern.

B Drop Quilt

This is a method for quilting on stitch lines in piecework or applique.

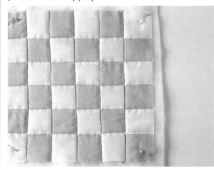

①Since this is done with walking foot, the feed dog is raised so the cloth is not pushed forward by hand, rather, it is pulled ahead naturally by sewing.

②Continue sewing between the piecework cloth

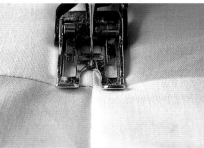

※When drop quilting in curved applique, free motion can be used if you know how to do it.

C Free Motion

This is a method for quilting a designed pattern onto a quilt.

By Machine, single line design is used for quilting. By combining two or three layers, this can also be made to seem like Hawaiian or echo-quilting.

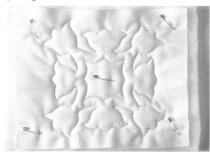

①After drawing the pattern on the cloth, attach lining to cotton using safety pins, and quilt from the center. When doing this, lower the feed dog and use the darning foot (quilting foot) as in the photo. Sew two or three times in one place and start, and do this again at the end.

②Without changing the direction of the cloth, move the line left and right under the needle by hand. Thimbles are very useful for this.

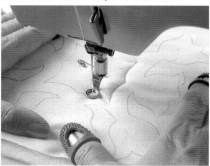

③Do not change the direction of the cloth.

④This method is very useful for single line patterns.

D Stipple Quilt
Two other types of free motion quilting are meander quilting and stipple quilting. Because the pattern is raised, this is often used for background quilting.

①Use the darning foot and lower the feed dog. Pulling the cloth with both hands, quilt in a meandering pattern, taking care not to cross the stitching.

[5] MAKE QUILT PATTERNS

①You can make your own quilting patterns easily. First, fold a paper in four or in half, and make your pattern.

②Cut along the line with scissors.

③Open it up.

④Pin pattern onto cloth and trace with French chalk.

⑤Finished!

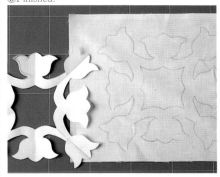

LESSON 7
USEFUL CREATIONS
NEAT THINGS FOR THE DRESSER

You'll enjoy dressing up with this white quilt for ladies. You'll be making all kinds of designs after mastering the rope basket technique.

LESSON 8

SCRAP QUILTS AND FINISHING THE QUILT

CHARM QUILT

①When you've gathered lots of cloth scraps, cut them to the same size and save them. You can make a neat quilt by using the scraps with new cloth. If there's only one piece left of each, it's called a "charm quilt". Master quilting by making this baby quilt.

②Materials; 62 pieces of scrap cloth 6 cm × 6 cm (2 3/8" × 2 3/8"), 124 pieces solid blue and pink cloth 6 cm × 6 cm (2 3/8" × 2 3/8"), 124 pieces 8 × 8 cm (3 1/8" × 3 1/8"). The blue cloth is the same size as the pink cloth, but is cut diagonally.

③Cut the blue and pink cloth diagonally.

④After cutting.

⑤Arrange around 6 cm (2 3/8") scrap cloth.

⑥The solid triangle is chain-stitched (directions on page 5) to the 6 cm (2 3/8") scrap.

⑦Stitch another triangle to the opposite side in the same way.

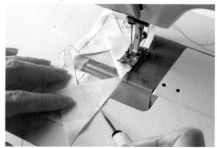

⑧Fold seam open after sewing triangles to both

⑨Next, sew triangles to other sides of the square.

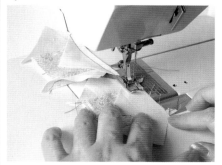

⑩Chain-stitched together.

⑪Fold open the seams and trim edges at 8 cm (3 1/8"). At this point, it is important that the square is centered and there is allowance for a 0.7

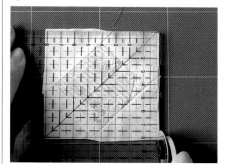

⑫Join the 8 cm (3 1/8") printed cloth to the cut

⑬This is also chain-stitched and opened up.

⑭Make 36 sets this way. Join these in turn into 4 sets of 18, and then sew them all together.

SCRAP QUILT FOR BABY

①After you've finished the scrap quilt, add a border. The border is a 4 cm (1 1/2") strip of pink cloth and a 9 cm (3 1/2") strip of patterned cloth. Attach lining, cotton, and cloth every 10-15 cm (4-6") with safety pins.

Making 45° corners:

❶Place the corner of border cloth A on top of cloth B and draw a 45° line.

❷Place the corner of border cloth B on top of cloth A and draw a 45° line.

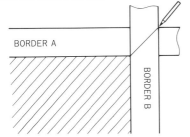

❸Match up lines ❶ and ❷ sew together, leaving a 0.7 cm (1/4") allowance, and cut.

❹ The corner is now 45°.

②Stitch from the center (refer to page 40). If the quilt is large, roll up both sides and hold using a clamp.

③Stitching has only been done on the outer four corners of the square and on both sides of the border.

④Attach binding. Make a strip 7 cm (2 3/4") wide and 10 cm longer than the outside edge. Fold in half and iron.

⑤Pin a double binding cloth a small distance from the corner.

⑥Sew a 0.7 cm (1/4") seam.

⑦Fold the corner and attach pins to both sides as in the photo.

⑧Sew ahead to the pins. Sew again and finish.

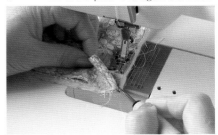

47

⑨Sew on the other side of the pin. Sew again and finish.

⑩After sewing all four corners like this, fold the last part and insert into the first part, and you're done sewing.

⑪Turn over and blind stitch the binding. Fold the corner as in the photo.

⑫Turn over. 45° line is finished.

⑬Fold back the left side of the back.

⑭Fold the right side over the left.

⑮Front side is 45°.

⑯Back side is also 45°.

⑰Blind stitch the back side.

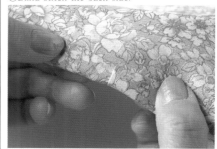

※Border corners can also be finished at 90°. This is easier than the 45° corner.

BORDER CLOTH

BORDER CLOTH

※To keep the edges of the quilt from bunching up, measure the top of the quilt and decide the size.
※The binding can be a single cloth. In order to finish precisely, use a bias cloth.
※It is difficult to make quilts in a small space, but bit can be done by making blocks and joining them together. This is called "Quilt as you go".

A New Baby Girl!

LESSON 8
USEFUL CREATIONS
GIFTS FOR INFANTS

Patchwork also means enjoying collecting
different types of cloth. Use all the soft
cotton cloth you've gathered to make this
quilt for baby.

BABY QUILT——Instructions on page 80
CARRYING BAG—Instructions on page 80

LESSON 9
PAPER PIECING

①In paper piecing, also called the paper foundation technique, a pattern is drawn on paper and the cloth and paper are sewn together. This is a fun technique for putting designs in small accessories and clothes.

②Once mastered, most of the four basic blocks shown in the photo can be expanded into a variety of creations.

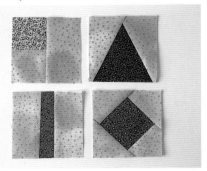

③Coordinated Fabrics   Japanese Rice Paper American books recommend using tracing paper or tissue paper. Japanese rice paper is suitable because it doesn't tear easily but thread passes through it easily, and it doesn't slip when attached to cloth.

④Trace the piecework pattern onto the rice paper. Leave 0.7 cm (1/4") allowance for seam around the border. Pieces should be cut 3 cm (1 1/4") in size.

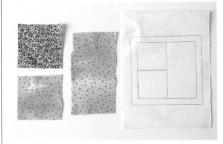

⑤Place the rough side of the paper on top of the front of the cloth.

⑥Join the next cloth inside-out to the first cloth.

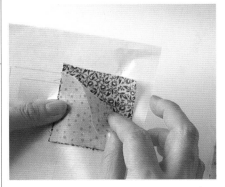

⑦Pin the cloth to the paper. Sew from mark to mark along the line on the paper. Fine stitching is necessary at the beginning and the end.

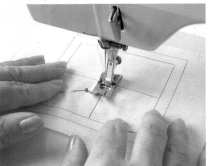

⑧After finished sewing, turn over. Trim the seam leaving 0.7 cm (1/4") allowance.

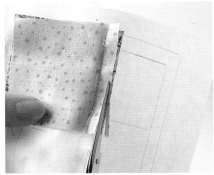

⑨Looks like this after opening.

⑩Join next cloth inside-out.

⑪Sew along line on paper as in step⑦. Trim the seam and open as in the photo.

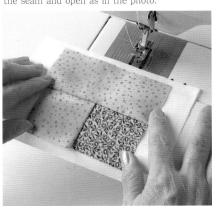

⑫Turn over cloth from step ⑪, place paper on top, trim along outside line.

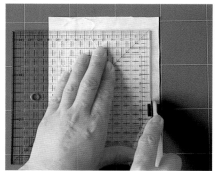

⑬After cutting. Include 0.7 cm (1/4") for seam.

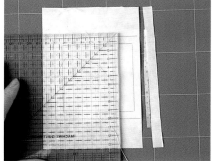

⑭Trim all of the edges.

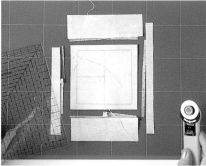

⑮Remove the paper.

⑯Piecework is done perfectly.

⑰This is the square-in-square pattern. Trim the cloth 3 cm (1 1/4") larger than the pattern.

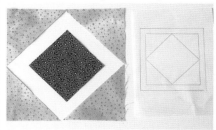

⑱Join the cloth inside-out to the back of the paper.

⑲Join the next piece inside-out too.

⑳Trim off allowance.

㉑Sewing is completed.

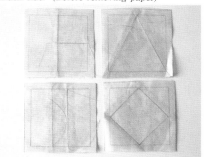

㉒Back side. (Before removing paper)

LESSON 9
USEFUL CREATIONS
HEARTFUL PRESENT

Looks like the tulips are in full bloom. And those must be terriers. These cute designs make adults and children alike happy.

LESSON 10
FOUR TECHNIQUES FOR STRIP PIECING

[1] SEMINOLE A

①The Seminole is the most popular strip piecing design. Named for the Native Americans of Florida, this design that uses three strips, is also the most basic.

②Cloth A: 4.5 cm × 110 cm (1 3/4" × 43") two pieces Cloth B: 4.5 cm × 110 cm (1 3/4" × 43"). Cut both sides of the entire length of the 110 cm (43") strip, allowing 1.5 cm (5/8") for seam.

③Sew strips together with a 0.7 cm (1/4") seam and iron. In this case, both sides of the seam are folded back.

④Cut into pieces 4.5 cm (1 3/4") wide.

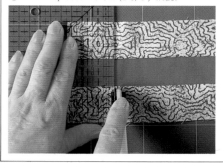

⑤Arrange as in photo.

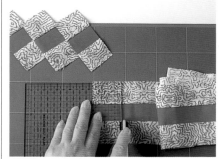

⑥Offset each piece one step and line up seams.

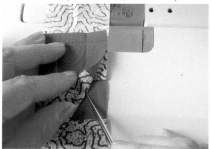

⑦Sew with 0.7 cm (1/4") seam.

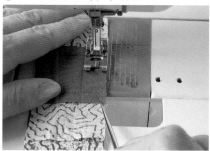

⑧Sew sections together one after another.

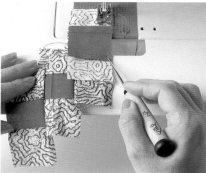

⑨After sewing all pieces together, iron cloth in one direction, as in photo.

⑩Trim 0.7 cm (1/4") outside of corners of square in center of cloth.

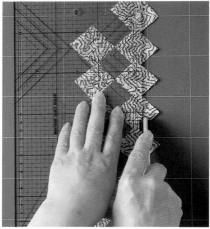

⑪Trimmed.

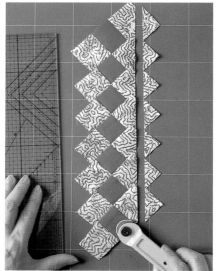

⑫Turn cloth and trim opposite side.

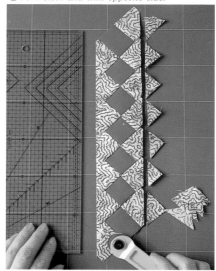

SEMINOLE B

①Have fun changing the width and angle of strips of the Seminole. In this design, the width changes.

②Cloth A: 5 cm × 110 cm (2" × 43") 2 pieces
Cloth B: 2.5 cm × 110 cm (1" × 43") 2 pieces
Cloth C: 3.5 cm × 110 cm (1 3/8"× 43") five pieces total

③Sew strips together with 0.7 cm.

④Trim a bit from the end and cut into pieces 4 cm (1 1/2") wide.

⑤Arrange the 4 cm (1 1/2") wide pieces as shown in the photo.

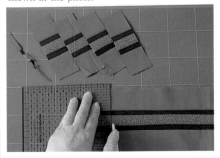

⑥Offset the seams, match the corners and sew together.

⑦Sew pieces on one after another.

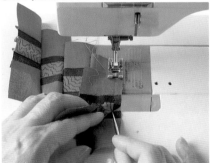

⑧Turn over and iron.

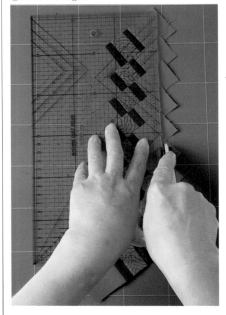

⑨Trim the edges.

⑩Completed trimming.

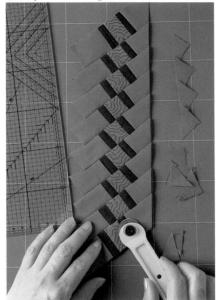

⑪Turn around and trim the other side.

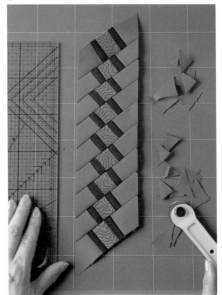

[2] SPIRAL

①This is made by twisting the cloth.

②Cut two pieces each of A, B, C, D, and E, 4.5 cm × 110 cm (1 3/4" × 43"). Arrange from the

③Line up the edges of two pieces of cloth and mark at 3.5 cm (1 3/8"). If the mark is made at a shorter point, the angle is shallower.

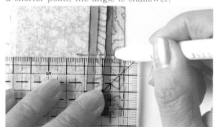

④Match up the next piece of cloth and piece together.

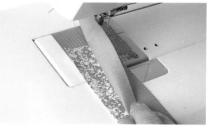

⑤Sew together, matching up the marks on the edge of the first cloth and the next cloth.

⑥A pair of cloths is made, as in the photo.

⑦Join the edge of the first cloth to the edge of

⑧Join the strips end to end and pin together. The cloth becomes twisted.

⑨With the cloth twisted thus, sew with a 0.7 cm

⑩Sew together while removing the pins.

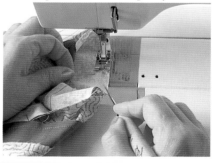

⑪The tubes are becoming stripes.

⑫You've made a twisted tube!

⑬Iron in one direction. Make two tubes with opposite stripes.

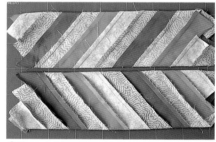

⑭Turned right-side out.

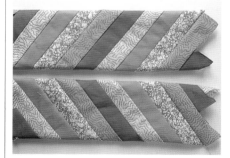

⑮Trim the edges from the front or back side.

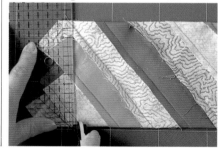

⑯After trimming.

⑰Cut into 4.5 cm (1 3/4") doughnut-shaped pieces.

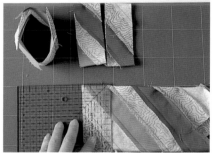

⑱After cutting both tubes.

⑲Separate the seam between the same pair of strips on all pieces.

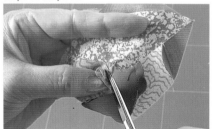

⑳Arrange the pairs.

㉑Sew pairs together to make a unit.

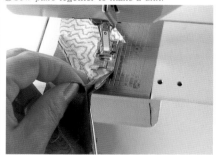

㉒Sew two pieces together at a time.

㉓Looks like photo.

㉔Iron after sewing all pieces together.

㉕Measure the length and width of the completed pattern. Trim edges straight.

㉖Finished cutting.

㉗Turn and trim other side.

ANOTHER SPIRAL DESIGN

Diamond (Basic Star)

When making a star from a spiral, do piecing in just one direction and cut. Offset one step, remove one seam, and sew together.

[3] BAJERO

①This pattern is used in Europe for needlepoint on chairs, and has been adapted to quiltwork. One piece is the same as one stitch in needlepoint. The photo shows strip piecing of pieces cut to the same length.

②By cutting to different widths, a curved effect can be created.

③Cut A, B, C, D, E, F, and G 4.5 cm × 110 cm (1 3/4" × 43")

④Strip piece together with a 0.7 cm (1/4") seam.

⑤Strip piecing is finished.

⑥Fold the seams down in one direction and iron.

⑦Strip piece the first and last strips to make a tube.

⑧It is now a tube.

⑨Place a ruler on the edge.

⑩Trim with a rotary cutter.

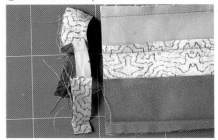

⑪Cut into 4.5 cm (1 3/4") doughnut-shaped pieces.

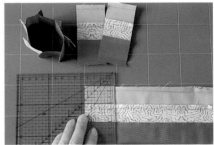

⑫Turn right-side out. Remove seam in one spot.

⑬Continue removing seam.

⑭When one seam is removed, remove the seam between the next pair of strips in the next piece, and arrange to make this offset pattern.

⑮Join pieces together.

⑯Back looks like this.

⑰Sew together, offsetting each piece one step.

⑱Iron the back like this.

[4] FRACTURE

①Placing strips in a large print yields a new effect. When inserting the strips, it's important that the pattern doesn't move.

②Cut off black strips and insert into print on the left. Consider balance when cutting the print.

③Back side.

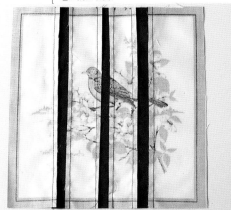

LESSON 10
USEFUL CREATIONS

TRAVEL BAGS

Whether you're going on vacation or just a small trip, you'll find these travel bags both versatile and extremely stylish.

LESSON 11
QUILT PRESSED BY STRINGS
(STRAIGHT DESIGN)

①In this method, the cloth is sewn directly onto the line. Quilting and piecing are done simultaneously. The strip is a long piece of new cloth, and "string" means a long unmatched piece of cloth.

②Lining (packing), batting, string; several types.

③Arrange the cloth on hand or use new cloth.

④Place the packing and batting on the first string, match up with the edge of the next string, and sew together.

⑤Turn over and turn the next string inside-out. Match the edge, sew together, and turn over.

⑥Repeat the same process.

⑦Repeat one more time.

⑧Batting is almost covered.

⑨Cut to required size using ruler and rotary cutter.

⑩After cutting.

⑪Cut border to required size.

⑫Back side

QUILT PRESSED BY STRINGS (WILD DESIGN)

①Patterns are not only done by pressed quilting on a line, but wild patterns can also be made by sewing pieces from the center as in this example.

⑤After this, sew at any angle desired and cut. Sew on the last cloth and cut.

⑥The required part is covered.

⑦Trim the edge and adjust the shape.

②Batting, packing, cloth; several types

③Place pieces around center cloth and sew on in a clockwise direction.

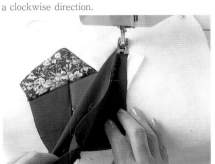

④When one circuit is completed, match cloth to center shape and cut.

⑧Back side

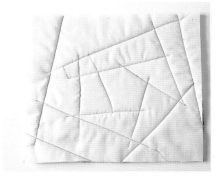

LESSON 11
USEFUL CREATIONS

HAVE FUN WITH THIS VEST

Are you enjoying machinework? How about having some fun making these stylish wearable creations.

VEST————Instructions on page 94 & 95
SMALL BAG————Instructions on page 93

INSTRUCTIONS FOR MAKING USEFUL CREATIONS

Yasuko Kuraishi's
Fun and Easy
MACHINEWORK AND QUILTWORK
Basic Techniques for Beginners

Before starting your project...

Do you ever use your sewing machine, or does it just sit there on the shelf looking sad?

Its charm is that it can sew fast, straight, and even. Learn the techniques of each lesson and start making your creation.

Big projects look difficult, but you can do them easily with a sewing machine. Choose your tools depending on the craft, It's fun to try making the crafts that come to you during the day. There is no end to the number of practical designs that you can make by sewing machine.

The photo shows a Holly Hobby applique. This patchwork for a dress is from lesson 1, Joining Squares by Machinework.

LUNCHEON MAT (LESSONS 1 & 2)

FROM PAGE 16

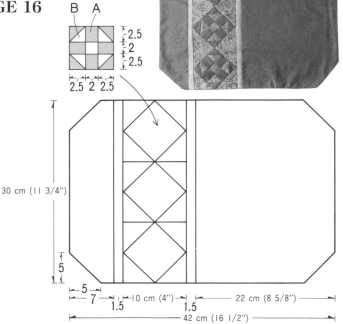

Finished Size 30 cm × 42 cm (11 3/4" × 16 1/2")

Materials (for one piece)

Front Cloth...A (green) 45 cm × 35 cm (17 3/4" × 13 3/4")

B (flower pattern) 35 cm × 15 cm (13 3/4" × 6") C (yellow) 35 cm × 5 cm (13 3/4" × 2") Lining green and beige check 45 cm × 35 cm (17 3/4" × 13 3/4")

Instructions

①Refer to Lessons 1 & 2 to make three sections of pattern block (chain dash) from front cloth A & B. (Draw squares on the paper according to the formula 2.5 cm + 2 cm + 0.7 cm = 5.2 cm (1" + 3/4" + 1/4" + 2 1/16") and join the triangles into a block, then make from front cloths A and B.) The triangles bordering the block are made by diagonally quartering a 15 cm × 15 cm (6" × 6") square of front cloth B.

②Attach 1.5 cm (5/8") strips along the right and left sides. Then attach a 7 cm (2 3/4") strip of front cloth A to the left side and a 22 cm (8 5/8") strip of A to the right side. Trim along a diagonal line 5 cm (2") inside the corner.

③Cut the lining to the same size as the front cloth and turn inside-out. Open in one place and sew. Turn right side-out, iron, and blind-stitch the opening.

BREAD BASKET COVER (LESSONS 1 & 2)

FROM PAGES 16 & 17

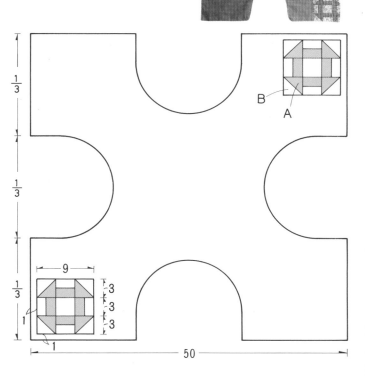

Finished Size Refer to Diagram

※Place in basket and fold corners over bread. Sew monkey wrench designs at the corners. To make this reversible, use the same design on the backs of the corners.

Materials

For monkey wrench cloth at corners:... A red check cloth B flower pattern cloth, 20 cm (8") square, each. Base Cloth...red and beige check cloth, green and beige check cloth 50 cm (19 3/4") square, each.

Instructions

①Trim a half-circle about one third from the center of each side, as in the diagram. Applique 9 cm (3 1/2") monkey wrench blocks to the corners. Refer to Lesson 2 for joining triangles in the monkey wrench blocks. draw squares on the paper according to the formula 3 cm + 2 cm + 0.7 cm + 5.7 cm (1 1/4" + 3/4" + 1/4" = 2 1/4"). To join the rectangles, strip piece 3 cm (1 1/4") pieces of cloth A and B cut at 4.5 cm(1 3/4"). Cut a 4.5 cm (1 3/4") square for the center cloth and join all pieces.

②After attaching monkey wrench applique to base cloth, turn right side-out and machine stitch around the outside.

TEA COZY (LESSONS 1 & 2) FROM PAGES 16 & 17

Finished Size 23 cm × 27 cm (9" × 10 5/8")
Materials
Front Cloth...A (flower pattern), B (green and beige check), C (red and beige check), adequate amounts of each.
Liner (small flower pattern) 30 cm × 50 cm (11 3/4" × 19 3/4")
Quilt cotton 30 cm × 50 cm (11 3/4" × 19 3/4") Sufficient medium yarn
Instructions
①Cut 9 cm (3 1/2") squares of front cloth A, B, and C. Join squares A and B, and A and C to make squares, as described in Lesson 1 until the desired size is reached.
②Join block made in step ①, place quilt cotton on lining and quilt using the drop quilt method described in Lesson 7. Cut two pieces of the necessary size.
③Cut front cloth 3 cm (1 1/4") on bias. Turn ② inside-out and insert the medium yarn, and sew together. At the same time, sew the handle into the top.
④Cut front cloth B 5 cm (2") on bias and finish the edge.

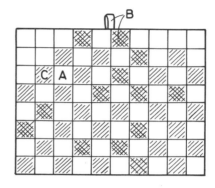

※MAKING BIAS TAPE

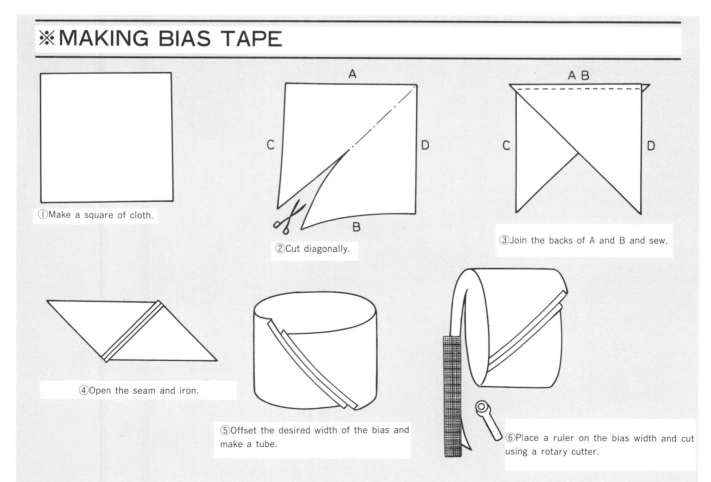

①Make a square of cloth.

②Cut diagonally.

③Join the backs of A and B and sew.

④Open the seam and iron.

⑤Offset the desired width of the bias and make a tube.

⑥Place a ruler on the bias width and cut using a rotary cutter.

BED COVER (LESSON 3)

FROM PAGES 22 & 23

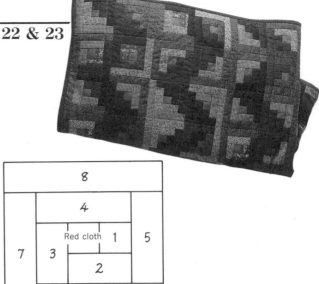

Finished size   220 cm × 140 cm (86 1/2" × 55")

Materials

Front Cloth...Red type, Brown type; Several pieces (refer to photo), joined width 114 cm × about 4 m (45" × 147.5")

Lining...flower print 114 cm × 280 cm (45" × 110")

Quilt cotton 240 cm × 160 cm (96" × 63")

Instructions

①Cut three hundred and eight 3.5 cm (1 3/8") squares of red cloth for the center. Cut the other cloth into 3.5 cm (1 3/8") strips. Refer to the Log Cabin in Lesson 3 to make three hundred and eight 10 cm (4") blocks.

②Arrange the blocks as desired. (Try to join bright and dark colors such as red and brown in this bed cover.)

③when the quilt top from step ② is completed, place the quilt cotton and lining onto it and attach with pins spaced 10 cm - 15 cm (4" - 6") apart. Stitch by drop quilting. (Refer to the Quilt in Lesson 8.)

④Fold 6 cm × 720 cm (15" × 283.5") binding cloth in half. Finish the edges by double binding. (Refer to Lesson 8 for instructions on attaching bindings.)

CUSHION (LESSON 4) FROM PAGE 28

[Eight -Pointed Star]

Finished size   40 cm (15 3/4") square

Materials

Front side...cloth (A, B, C) adequate amount, refer to photo

Back side...navy blue cloth 42 cm × 48 cm (16 1/2" × 19")

Lining...white cloth 42 cm (16 1/2") square

Quilt cotton 42 cm (16 1/2") square, 36 cm (14 1/4") zipper, plain cushion

Instructions

①Draw a 40 cm 16(") square on paper, and then refer to Lesson 4 and draw an eight-pointed star in this. Make three patterns, for diamonds, triangles, and squares, based on this pattern.

②Quarter the diamond pattern. Measure the length of one side.

③Piece two strips of width determined by adding 1.5 cm (5/8") allowance and 0.5 cm (3/16") (surplus) to measurement from step ②.   Cut at 45° and then cut again to make eight diamond-shaped pieces.

④Place the pattern paper on the cut diamond shapes and arrange the shapes leaving a 0.7 cm (1/4") seam. Refer to the Eight-Pointed Star in Lesson 4 and sew together.

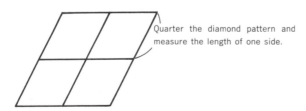

Quarter the diamond pattern and measure the length of one side.

⑤After finishing the quilt top from step ④, attach quilt cotton and lining with pins. Refer to Quilting in Lesson 7 and stitch by drop quilting. Trim of excess parts.

⑥Attach zipper to back side of the cloth and shape into a cushion. (Refer to page 90)

※If you wish to make the cushion the same size as the materials, the surplus from step ③ is needed.

[HEAVENLY STAR]

Finished size 40 cm (15 3/4") square

Materials

Front side...cloth (A, B, C) adequate amount, refer to photo

Back side...red cloth 42 cm × 48 cm (16 1/2" × 19")

Lining...white cloth 42 cm (16 1/2") square

Quilt cotton 42 cm (16 1/2") square, 36 cm (14 1/4") zipper, Plain cushion

Instructions

①Draw a 40 cm (16") square on paper and divide this into quarters. Draw 20 cm (8") squares in the center of this. Draw eight-pointed stars in each of the squares. (Refer to Eight-Pointed Star in Lesson 4.)

②Make a pattern as shown on the right. Make the pattern and cut the necessary pieces of cloth.

③Refer to lesson 4 and join the stars and squares.

④Pin the quilt top from step ③ to the quilt cotton and lining.

⑤Attach the zipper to the back side of the cloth and finish the cushion.

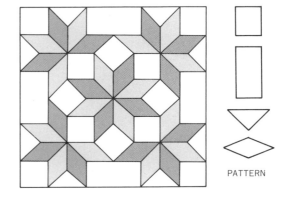

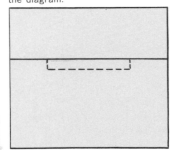

PATTERN

Attaching the Zipper

①Cut 6 cm (2 3/8") from just one side of the quilt top.

②Fold 3 cm (1 1/4") from the long side of both cloths.

③Place the zipper on both sides of the fold line in step ② and blind stitch.

④Offset the closed section and cut.

⑤Fold the shorter part and short side 3 mm (1/8"), and attach the zipper.

⑥Turn inside-out and sew as in the diagram.

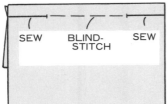

SEW   BLIND-STITCH   SEW

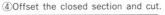

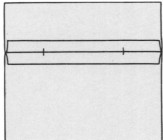

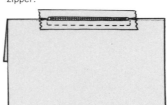

TAPESTRY (LESSON 4) FROM PAGE 29

[Variable Star Small Quilt]

Finished size 146 cm × 118 cm (57 1/2" × 46 1/2")

Materials

Front Cloth...A (navy blue), B (red), C (small flower pattern), D (white cotton) sufficient amount.

Lining...white cotton sheeting 114 cm × 175 cm (45" × 69")

Quilting cotton 114 cm × 135 cm (57 1/2" × 53")

Instructions

①Make eighteen 18 cm (7") (19.5 cm (7 1/2") including seam) sawtooth star blocks using front cloths A, B, and C. (Refer to Lesson 4; Star Variations)

②Cut seventeen 19.5 cm (7 1/2") squares from front cloth D.

③Join ① and ②.

④Attach front cloth B 3 cm (1 1/4"), D 5 cm (2"), and A 4 cm (1 1/2") to the margin. Make a border. (Refer to Lesson 8; Attaching the Border).

⑤Refer to Lesson 7; Quilting, and Lesson 8; Finishing the Quilt and finish as in the photo.

※Make grommets from sheeting.

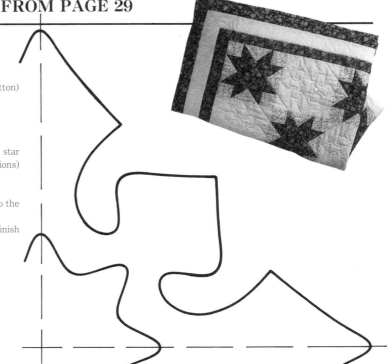

TAPESTRY AND FRAME (LESSON 5) FROM PAGE 34

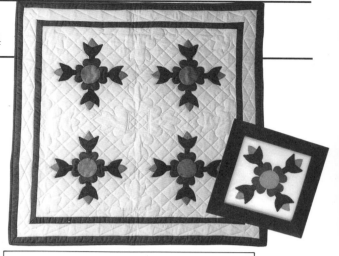

[Ohio Star Christmas Quilt]

Finished size 64 cm (25") square
Materials
Front Cloth...A (red), B (yellow), C (green) adequate amounts of each D (white) 110 cm × 100 cm (43" × 39 1/2")
Lining... white cotton sheeting 65 cm × 85 cm (25 1/2" × 33 1/2")
Quilting cotton 64 cm (25") square
Instructions
①Cut five 19.5 cm (7 3/4") squares of front cloth. Refer to the blind stitch applique in lesson 5 to make four blocks from four of these squares.
②Make a 31 cm (12 1/4") square of front cloth D, cut this diagonally, and attach on four corners.
③Cut two 22 cm (8 3/4") squares of front cloth D, cut each of these diagonally, and join these at the top and bottom and to the left and right. Refer to the photo.
④Trim the edge leaving a 0.7 cm (1/4") seam.
⑤Attach a 1.5 cm (1/2") wide strip to the edge of the block from step ④. Attach front cloth D (4 cm (1 1/2") wide) and sew onto front cloth A (2.5 cm (1") wide, and finish as a frame. Cut all of this with a seam allowance.
⑥Quilt and finish by binding.
※For the quilting diagram, refer to the Folded Paper Method .
⑦Insert the stick into the reverse side.

[Frame]

Finished size 25 cm (10") square (frame width 3.5 cm (1 1/4"))
Materials
Cloth A (red), B (yellow), C (green) small amount of each, D (white) 19 cm × 19 cm (7 1/2" ×7 1/2")
Instructions
①Use one Ohio Rose in a tapestry, blind stitch, applique, and put in frame.

WREATH (LARGE, SMALL) (LESSON 5)   FROM PAGE 34

[Holly Wreath]

Finished size   (Large) diameter ~ 31 cm (12") (Small) ~ 20 cm (8")

Materials

holly leaves...cloth A (Christmas green), B (green tree pattern) sufficient amounts of each

red berries...a small amount of red cloth, a small amount of cotton, wreath base...cloth A (Christmas green) 30 cm × 60 cm (12" × 23 1/2")

velvet ribbon...large wreath; 4 cm (1 1/2") wide 110 cm (43 1/2")   small wreath; 2.5 cm (1") wide 65 cm (25 1/2")

Domit cotton, Green thread

Instructions

①Draw as many holly leaves as needed on cloth A and B.

②Place the domit cotton onto the cloth from step ① and pin in place. Machine stitch with green thread around the holly leaves, referring to the satin stitch applique in Lesson 5. The veins are straight-stitched (do the same for cloth B).

③Cut around the stitches after sewing.

④Draw a circle onto the wreath base cloth. Outside diameter is 29 cm (11 1/2") and inside diameter is 17 cm (6 3/4"). Place the domit cotton and cloth A onto the base cloth, satin stitch the inside diameter, and then cut it out. Make thirteen stitches around the outside diameter of the circle, satin stitch to the outside diameter and then cut it out. (This now has a donut-shape)

⑤Arrange the holly leaves from step ③ as shown in the photo and sew in place.

⑥Make twenty-one holly berries from the red cloth and sew onto the holly leaves as shown in the photo.

※For the holly berries, cut circles of red cloth, fold the edges, and insert the cotton as you sew.

⑦Attach bow to the top of the wreath.

※Make the small wreath from the remaining piece of base cloth. (Width of base is 4 cm (1 1/2")

※Domit cotton is stiff cotton, also called batting. It is used to stiffen crafts.

HOLLY LEAF AND BERRY (ACTUAL SIZE)

ORNAMENT (TREE , BOOT, WALL HANGING,) (LESSON 5)   FROM PAGE 35

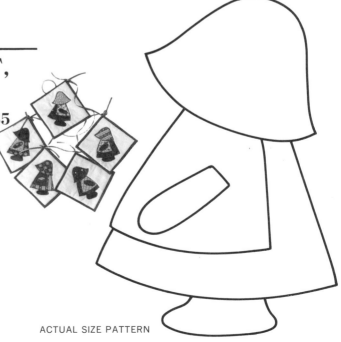

[Sue Bonnet Ornament]

Finished size   12 cm (4 3/4") square

Materials

Several types of Christmas print cloth, White cloth, Red cloth; adequate amounts of each,

Quilt cotton 36 cm × 24 cm (14 1/4" × 9 1/2") red ribbon 0.4 cm (1/8") wide, 260 cm (102"), Red thread

Instructions

①Consider the desired effect and cut the Sue pattern from the Christmas print. (It is interesting to reverse the pattern to make different ornaments).

②Make blocks as in the applique in Lesson 5, using the red cloth for the border.

③Decorate with a ribbon as in the photo.

ACTUAL SIZE PATTERN

[Tree]

Finished size   28 cm (11") high

Materials

Christmas green cloth; adequate amount

Domit cotton, Green thread, 3 large bells, 18 small bells

Instructions

①Draw three tree shapes onto the front side of the cloth.

②Place the domit cotton onto the cloth from step ①, place another piece of cotton on this, and pin in place. Machine stitch with green thread around the tree, referring to the satin stitch applique in Lesson 5. Using scissors, cut around the stitches after sewing.

③Place the three finished trees from step 2 on top of each other and carefully machine stitch along the center line.

④Sew the three large bells to the top of the tree and the small bells along the sides of the tree.

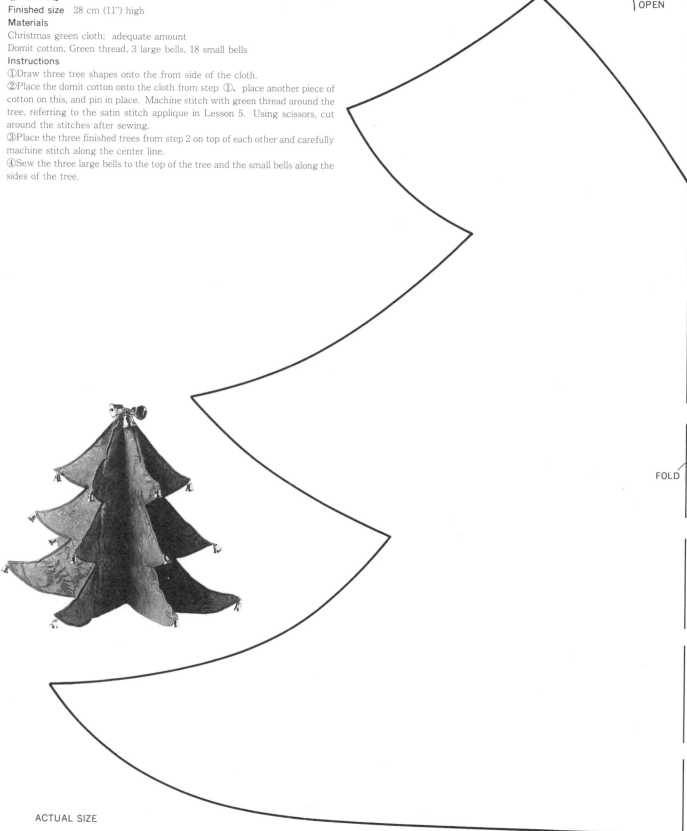

OPEN

FOLD

ACTUAL SIZE

[Boot]

Finished size   Refer to actual size pattern

※This uses Joining the Squares from Lesson 1 and Quilt Pressed by Strings from Lesson 11.

Materials

Christmas print cloth ; several types

Quilt cotton, 2 bells, Ribbon 0.4 cm (1/8") wide 40 cm (16")

Instructions

①Make a band of joined squares around the center. Cut 7 cm (2 3/4") squares from two types of Christmas print. Refer to Joining the Squares in Lesson 5 and join the squares into four blocks. Attach each at the top and bottom to the plain red cloth every 5.5 cm (2 1/4"), so that the corners match. This makes a 7.5 cm (3") wide band.

②Draw the boot shape onto the quilt cotton. Cut 1 cm (3/8") larger than needed. (Make two pieces for the opposing sides.) Match the pattern to position the band from step ① in the center. Refer to the Quilt Pressed by Strings in Lesson 11, and piece together. (Piecing is easy if you draw a line on the quilt cotton).

③Cut two pieces of lining in opposite directions the same size as in step ②.

④Join two pieces of front cloth and two pieces of lining inside-out. Carefully sew four pieces along the dotted line as in the diagram. Sew the front and lining separately above the dotted line.

⑤Turn right side-out to make a boot with lining.

⑥Sew bias around the top of the boot.

⑦Attach the ribbon and bell as in the photo.

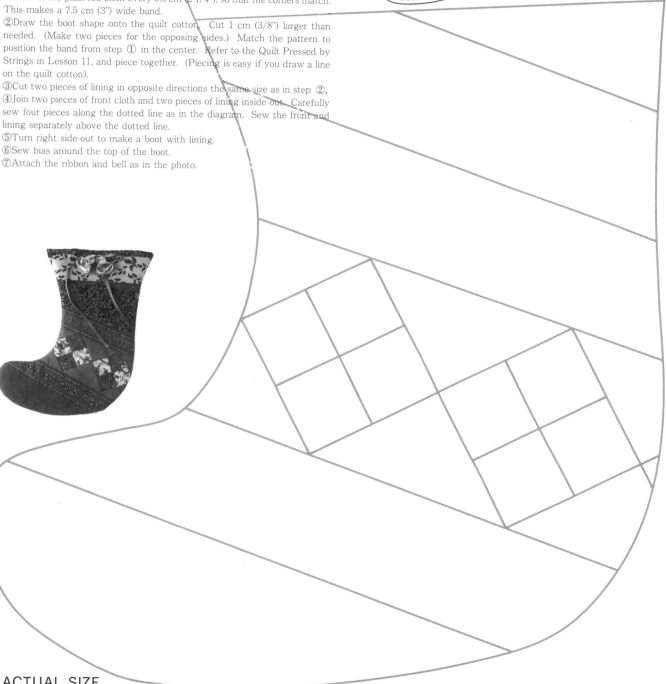

ACTUAL SIZE

TOTE BAG (LESSON 6) FROM PAGES 36 & 37

Finished size   width 36 cm (14") depth 30 cm (12")
Materials
Cloth A (black) 45 cm × 75 cm (18" × 29 1/2"), B (white pin stripes on black) 35 cm × 25 cm (14" × 10"), Domit cotton 100 cm × 50 cm (40" × 19 1/2") cotton; small amount
Instructions
①Strip piece one 3.5 cm (1 1/2") wide strip of cloth A to two 3.5 cm (1 1/2") wide strips of cloth B. Refer to the Square in Square in Lesson 6 and make two blocks.
②Join the two blocks and attach a 5.5 cm (2 1/4") wide strip of cloth A to the top, a 7.5 cm (3") strip of cloth A to the bottom, and a 2 cm (3/4") strip of cloth A to each side. Attach an 11 cm (4 1/4") wide piece of cloth B to each side of the block. Position the quilting cotton and lining and quilt. (The front is finished).
③Join cloth for the back side in the pattern: B, A, B, A, B, as shown in the diagram. Attach domit cotton and quilt. (Refer to Lesson 7).
④Cut two pieces of cloth the same size as cloth A for the bag lining.
⑤Cut two strips each of cloth A; 10 cm × 48 cm (4" × 19"), and cloth B; 5 cm × 48 cm (2" × 19"), for the handle. Insert cotton into the handle to make a 5 cm (2") wide strap, as seen in the diagram.
⑥Make into a bag. Turn the front side, back side and the section from step

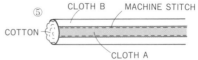

⑤ CLOTH B   MACHINE STITCH
COTTON
CLOTH A

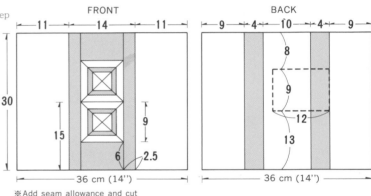

FRONT

| 11 | 14 | 11 |

30

15   9   6   2.5

36 cm (14")

BACK

| 9 | 4 | 10 | 4 | 9 |

8
9
12
13

36 cm (14")

※ Add seam allowance and cut

RUCKSACK (LESSON 6) FROM PAGES 36 & 37

Finished size   width 31 cm (12 1/4") depth 37 cm (14 1/2")
Materials
Cloth A (black) 100 cm × 50 cm (39 1/2" × 20"), B (white pinstripes on black) 100 cm × 50 cm (39 1/2" × 20").
Domit cotton 0.7 cm (1/4") thick black cord 150 cm (59"), Black velcro; small amount
Instructions
①Front side...Make a design as in the diagram, quilt domit cotton and lining. Back side...Quilt domit cotton and lining the same size as front cloth A. Cover...The block in the center is the same size as the tote bag. Sew as shown in the
diagram.Attach lining cloth (A) to bag, turn over and finish in the back. Gusset...Join quilt cotton and lining and machine quilt every other centimeter 1 cm (3/8").
Strap...Prepare two straps the same width as the tote bag and 70 cm (27 1/2")long
②Finish as a rucksack. Turn the front of the bag and the gusset inside-out, tightly sew everything except the opening. Sew the other end of the gusset to the back of the bag. Insert the strap into the indicated place and sew tightly. (Use cloth A for the bias and clean up the allowance.) Trim the excess from the ends of the gussets and align them. Wrap the opening with 3 cm (1 1/4") wide cloth B bias tape and make an opening for the cord. Attach the lid to the back side (now attach the strap to the indicated position and sew). Sew velcro to the front to make a closure. Pass the cord through the opening.

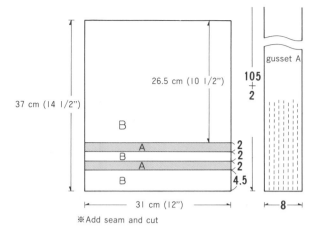

37 cm (14 1/2")

26.5 cm (10 1/2")

B

A

B

A

B

2
2
2
4.5

31 cm (12")

※Add seam and cut

105 + 2

gusset A

8

5
3
Attach lid here
1
5 1 7 3
Attach strap here

A

1

3

Attach strap here

4 5 13 cm (5") 5 4

26

A

10

B

26

13

15 cm (6")

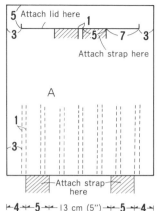

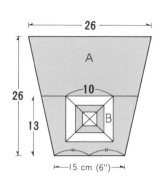

BASKET LINER (LESSON 7) FROM PAGE 43

Finished size In this case 20 cm × 25 cm (8" × 10") for 8 cm (3 1/4") high basket

Materials

White cloth 90 cm × 105 cm (35 1/2" × 41 1/2") Lining 90 cm × 105 cm (35 1/2" × 41 1/2")

Thin quilting cotton 45 cm × 52 cm (18" × 20")

1.7 cm (5/8") wide Tyrolean tape and 2 cm (3/4") wide white lace, each 140 cm (55"), 1.3 cm (1/2")wide pink satin ribbon 150 cm (59"), White quilt thread

Instructions

①Make a pattern the size of the basket, and cut the quilt cotton and cloth to match this pattern.

②Place quilt cotton and white cloth on the cloth from step ① and, referring to Lesson 7, quilt a 3 cm (1 1/4") checker pattern.

③Satin stitch the edge and finish.

④Attach lace and Tyrolean tape at the four sides, as shown in the photo.

Make bows from the ribbon and attach at the four corners.

TISSUE CASE (LESSON 7) FROM PAGE 43

Finished size Same as typical tissue box

Materials

White cloth, small flower pattern quilting cloth (lining) 40 cm × 35 cm (19" × 14") each.

Thin quilt cotton 40 cm × 35 cm (19" × 14") 1.7 cm (5/8") wide Tyrolean tape 110 cm (43"), 2 cm (3/4") wide lace 75 cm (29 1/2"), White quilt cotton

Instructions

①Make a pattern and cut white cotton, small flower pattern, and quilt cotton as shown. (Becareful to cut off enough pieces)

②Place white cloth, and quilt cotton on the lining and quilt a 3 cm (1 1/4") checker pattern onto this.

③Cut the opening of the tissue box and satin stitch around it. Attach Tyrolean tape to the opening.

④Sew into box shape and satin stitch the edge.

⑤Decorate the sides with Tyrolean tape and lace. (refer to the photo)

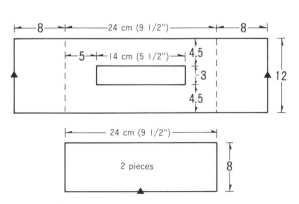

8 24 cm (9 1/2") 8

5 14 cm (5 1/2") 4.5
3
4.5

12

24 cm (9 1/2")

2 pieces

8

※ ▲ =Cut off without folding, 0.7 cm (1/4") seam

MAKE UP CAPE (LESSON 7)

FROM PAGE 43

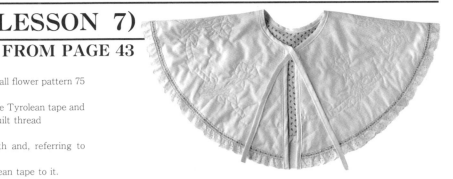

Finished size refer to diagram

Materials

White cloth 75 cm (29 1/2") square, Cream cloth with small flower pattern 75 cm (29 1/2") square (lining)

Thin quilt cotton 75 cm (29 1/2") square, 1 cm (3/8") wide Tyrolean tape and 2 cm (3/4") wide white lace each 200 cm (79") White quilt thread

Instructions

①Place thin cotton quilting and lining onto white cloth and, referring to Quilting in Lesson 7, quilt rose and spade.

②Insert lace between front and back, and attach Tyrolean tape to it.

③Attach bias tape to front edge and around neck, and finish.

Rose and Spade Diagram (Actual Size)

62 cm (24 1/2")

24 cm (9 1/2") 7

30

2 cm (3/4") wide lace

1 cm (3/8") wide Tyrolean tape

open

DOILY (LESSON 7) FROM PAGE 42

[White Quilt Doily]

Finished size 40 cm (16") square

Materials

White quilt cloth 40 cm × 100 cm (16" × 39"), Quilt cotton 40 cm (16")
square , White quilt thread

Instructions

①Copy diagram onto cloth.
②Quilt by referring to Lesson 7.
③Attach binding to edge.

White Quilt

Step Quilt

(Actual Size)

TECHNIQUES AND PATTERNS FOR QUILTING DESIGN

●With a sewing machine you can do quilting quickly and artistically. Refer to the following diagrams when selecting quilting design. (The quilting foot and walking foot attachments are very useful).

Drop Quilt

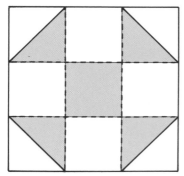

Outline Quilt

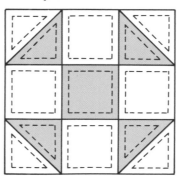

Kitty-Corner Checker Quilt

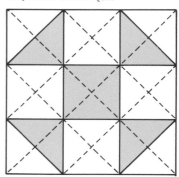

Combined Outline and Kitty-Corner

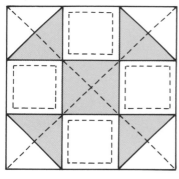

Continuous Design

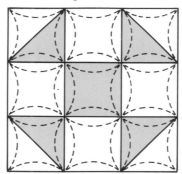

Motif Quilt

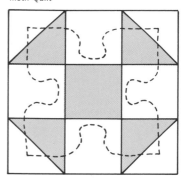

Echo Quilt

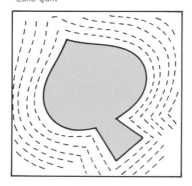

Quilting From the Inside to the Outside

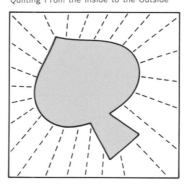

Stipple Quilt

ROPE BASKET (LESSON 7) FROM PAGE 42

Finished size bottom; major axis of oval 24 cm (9 1/2") depth 8 cm (3 1/4")

※ Rope

Tools...tube turner
Materials
long bias cloth (thickness of cord depends on width) Glue for cloth

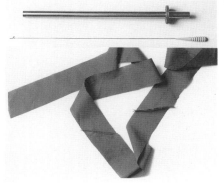

※ With this technique, you can make any basket you like. It's also fun to try changing the thickness of the rope.

Instructions

① Fold the bias cloth in two, machine stitch the edge so that the cord will fit inside.

② Insert the tube turner into the tube from 1 until the bias is full.

③ Insert the cotton cord into the tip. Insert a wire from the bottom until it hooks up with the cord, and then pull. The bias comes out inside-out at the same time.

④ When it is almost all out, cut the cord and slowly pull the wire.

⑤ Attach bias to the ring and follow the same steps from step ②. Put glue on the end of the bias tape. Insert taped cord into the opening. Pull from the opposite side.

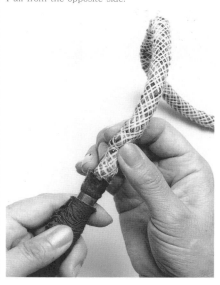

⑥ Continue step ⑤ and make a long rope with a cord inside.

※ Basket

Instructions

① Sew between the ropes with a teflon-coated wire using a zigzag stitch. Make the bottom of the basket first.

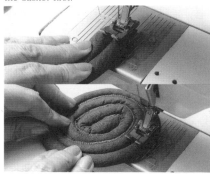

② After sewing the bottom into shape, hold the left side of the basket and sew between the ropes again with a zigzag stitch. At the end, fold the end of one rope into the previous rope, trying to finish the basket with an even look.

BABY QUILT (LESSON 8) FROM PAGES 48 & 49

Finished size 100 cm × 100 cm (39" × 39")
Materials
Front Cloth...A (many scraps) B(pink and blue, each 50 cm × 100 cm (19 1/2" × 39"), C (flower pattern 100 cm × 110 cm (39" × 43")
Lining Cloth...cream with small flower pattern 100 cm × 100 cm (39" × 39")
Quilt cotton 100 cm × 100 cm (39" × 39")
White quilt thread
Instructions
①Refer to Scrap Quilt in Lesson 8 and make seventy two square-in-square blocks (8 cm × 8 cm (3 1/4" × 3 1/4") with seam) from cloth A and B. Cut seventy two (8 cm × 8 cm (3 1/4" × 3 1/4") pieces of cloth C and sew these in sequence. Attach a 3.5 cm (1 3/8") wide strip of cloth B (pink) around the outside. Attach a 9.5 cm (3 3/4") wide strip of cloth C around the outside to make the quilt top.
②Refer to Finishing the Quilt to finish.

CARRYING BAG (LESSON 8) FROM PAGES 48 & 49

Finished size bag width 42 cm (16 1/2"), depth 42 cm (16 1/2")
Materials
Cloth A (nine pieces of scrap), B (blue and pink), C (small flower pattern) adequate amount
Lining... Pink cloth 45 cm × 90 cm (17 1/2" × 35 1/2")
Quilt cotton 50 cm × 100 cm (19 1/2" × 39") White quilt thread
Instructions
①Refer to Lesson 8 and make nine 8 cm × 8 cm (3 1/4" × 3 1/4") square-in-square blocks from cloth A and B.
②Attach a triangle of cloth C to the top and bottom of each block as in the diagram. Join the pieces together to make one piece.
③Cut two 5 cm (2") wide strips of cloth B and attach one to each side of step ②. Cut two 15 cm (6") wide strips of cloth C and attach one to each side of this. Place the quilt cotton and quilt liner on top, as shown in the diagram. (Refer to Quilting in Lesson 7)
④Handle. Cut two 10 cm × 70 cm (4" × 27 1/2") strips of cloth C and two strips cloth B 5 cm x 70 cm (2" × 27 1/2"). Sew with quilting cotton as in the diagram.
⑤Finishing the bag. Cut the lining the same size as the front in step ③. Turn front cloth and lining inside-out. Attach the handles between the sides (Try to make sure cloth B is in front) only sew the grasping section of the handle.
⑥Fold the center of the front and back separately, leave open in one spot and sew. (The handle must attach in the middle). Sew the gusset of the front and lining.
⑦Turn inside-out, insert the lining bag into the front bag, and finish the opening at last.

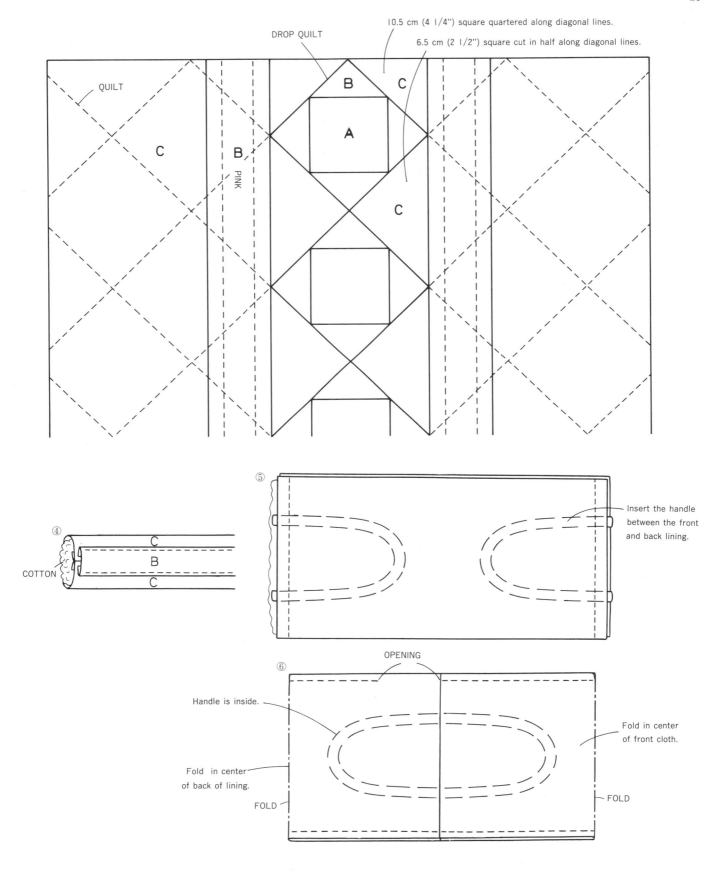

DROP QUILT

10.5 cm (4 1/4") square quartered along diagonal lines.

6.5 cm (2 1/2") square cut in half along diagonal lines.

QUILT

B

C

A

C

C

B

PINK

④

COTTON

C
B
C

⑤

Insert the handle
between the front
and back lining.

⑥

OPENING

Handle is inside.

Fold in center
of front cloth.

Fold in center
of back of lining.

FOLD

FOLD

PUPPY BAG (LESSON 7) FROM PAGE 52

Finished size   bag width 28 cm (11") depth 27 cm (10 1/2")

Materials

Cloth A (2-3 kinds for dog) B (base cloth, lining, handle) Plaid sufficient amount backing cloth

Instructions

①Make four blocks with dog pattern by paper piecing method. (Actual size pattern on page 84).

②Join the blocks from step 1 as in the diagram, attach quilt cotton and backing cloth, and quilt.

③cut handle from cloth B 30 cm × 5 cm (12" × 2"). Make two handles by the same method as the handles for the Tulip Bag.

④Cut lining from B the same size as in step ②.

⑤Sew both sides with a 0.7 cm (1/4") seam. A 9 cm (3 1/2") gusset must be sewn in the bottom corner. (Refer to diagram).

⑥Insert the inner bag into the outside bag and sew it onto the gusset. (Refer to diagram).

⑦Straighten out the outside and inside bag. Insert the handle from step ③ and sew tightly in place.

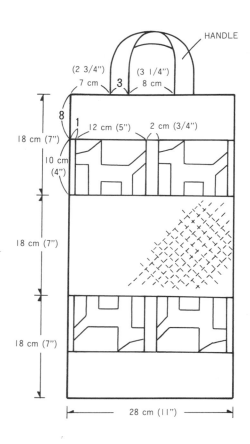

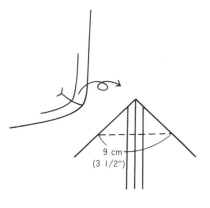

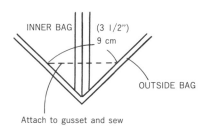

TULIP BAG (LESSON 9) FROM PAGE 52

Finished size bag width 33 cm (13") depth 26 cm (10")

Materials

Cloth A (4 types for tulips), Cloth B (base cloth, handle), Backing cloth, Lining adequate amounts of each, Quilt cotton 100 cm (39") square

Instructions

①Make six tulip blocks from cloth A by the paper piecing method. (Refer to Lesson 9). (Actual size pattern on page 85).

②Join pieces together with cloth B as in the diagram.

③Attach quilt cotton and backing cloth to step ②, quilt, and trim the edges.

④Make two 33 cm × 11.5 cm (13" × 4 1/2") handles from cloth B. Fold in center and wrap around the quilt cotton. Fold the edges inward 0.7 cm (1/4") each to make 33 cm × 5 cm (13" × 2") handles. Quilt four straight lines along the edges and inside of the handles. Fold 10 cm (4") of the center in half and sew. (A narrower handle makes it easier to carry).

⑤Cloth B, quilt cotton, and lining should be cut a bit larger than the bottom pattern. Quilt on a lattice.

⑥Cut the lining the same size as in steps ③ and ⑥.

⑦Attach the bottom to the front and sew the sides.

⑧Attach the bottom to the lining and sew the sides. This time, cut the seams (0.5 cm (3/16") larger.

⑨Sew the opening . Insert the handles between the inner and outer bag. Machine stitch 1 cm (3/8") from the opening and straighten out the bag.

※It is convenient to add an inner pocket (12 cm × 15 cm (5" × 6")) to the bag.

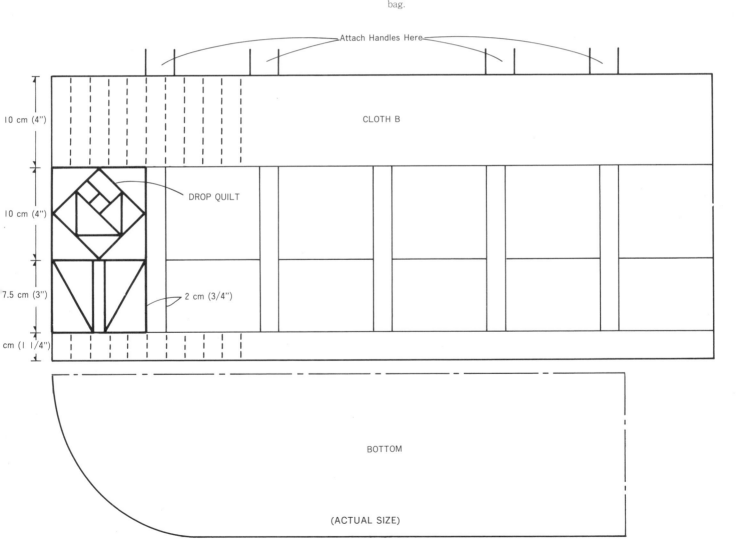

DIAGRAM FOR PAPER PIECING ACTUAL SIZE

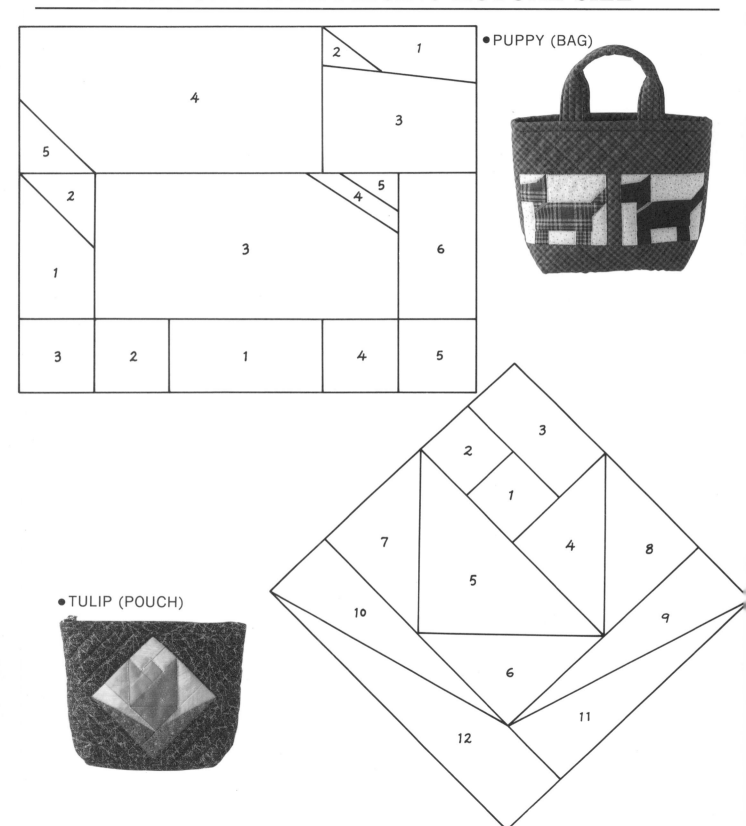

● PUPPY (BAG)

● TULIP (POUCH)

※ Piece from number I
※ If there are many same numbers in the diagram, take them apart and then join them.
※ If the diagram has a direction, trace it in the opposite direction.

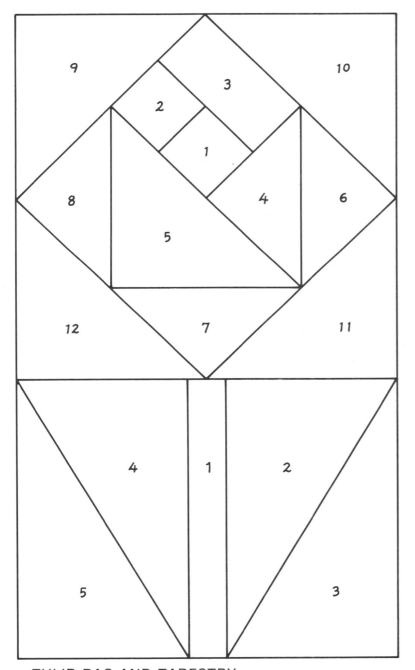

● TULIP BAG AND TAPESTRY

TULIP POUCH (LESSON 9) FROM PAGE 52

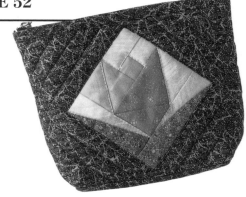

Finished size   width 18 cm (7") depth 15 cm (6")
Materials
Cloth A (four types for tulips), Cloth B (base cloth), Backing cloth Bias (4 cm (1 1/2") wide made of cloth B), small amount of quilt cotton, 20 cm (8") zipper
Instructions
①Make two tulip blocks using paper piecing. (Actual size pattern on page 84)
②Sew a 10 cm (4") wide strip of cloth B around the block. (Refer to diagram)
③Make two of these units and trim to 19 cm × 21 cm (7 1/2" × 8 1/4").
④Sew 5.5 cm (2 1/4") wide piece of cloth B between the units from step 3, place quilt cotton and backing on top and quilt. (Quilt five lines 1 cm (3/8") apart on the bottom)
⑤Sew both sides together, pinch four centimeters for the gusset and sew.
⑥Sew bias (finished width 1 cm (3/8")) to the opening and attach zipper.

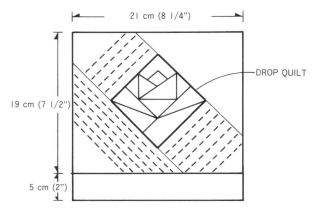

BALANCING MACHINE STITCHES AND THREAD

Every type of sewing machine has a tension block for the bobbin and thread. The tension block works by increasing or decreasing the tension of the thread as it passes through. If the pressure is too high, the stitches will be pulled out, and if it is too weak, the cloth will be too loose. In each of these, the stitching looks messy and weak. The best condition for the thread is to keep both side balanced and to stitches to reach center of the cloth. (Refer to page 4 about tension)

Upper Thread is Too Strong
The interlocking circle will come out on the upper cloth. This happens if the upper thread is too tight or the bobbin is too weak.

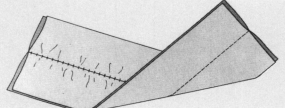

Upper Thread is Too Weak
The interlocking circle will come out on the lower cloth. This happens if the upper thread is too loose or the bobbin is too strong. Make sure to try to sew

Correct Thread Condition,
Keep the thread and bobbin balanced. Stitches should form an interlocking circle at the thickest point in the center of the cloth.

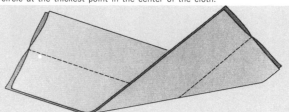

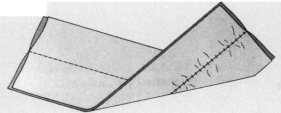

TULIP WALL HANGING (LESSON 9) FROM PAGE 53

Finished size 132 cm × 83 cm (52" × 33")

Materials

Cloth A (four types for tulips) small amount, Cloth B (border type) 150 cm × 50 cm (59" × 20") lining 140 cm × 90 cm (55" × 35 1/2")
Quilt cotton 140 cm × 90 cm (55" × 35 1/2")

Instructions

①Make thirty tulip blocks by paper piecing. (Actual size pattern is on page 85) Sew a lattice between these as in the diagram.
②Make a border as shown in the diagram.
③Attach quilt cotton and lining to block from step ② and quilt. Finish by binding.

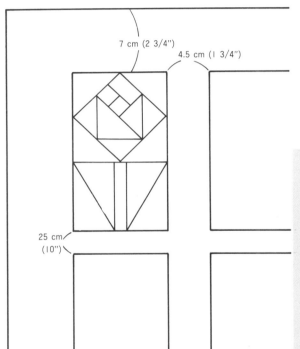

7 cm (2 3/4")

4.5 cm (1 3/4")

25 cm (10")

HOBBY CORNER

Nylon thread can be used in quilting and blind stitching to create the same effect as hand stitching. When doing this the thread can be taken off of the spool, but if the spool is just put into a jar, the thread comes out smoothly, and work can be done more quickly. A small idea makes sewing enjoyable and efficient.

TRAVEL BAG (LESSON 10)

FROM PAGE 60

Finished size bag width 55 cm (21 1/2") depth 33 cm (13")

Materials

Spiral cloth (7.5 cm × 110 cm (3" × 43") make two pairs of five spirals is one set. Two sets are needed, one each for the front and the back. solid brown cloth, backing cloth and lining; adequate amounts of each.

Quilt cotton 100 cm × 100 cm (39" × 39") 50 cm (19 1/2") zipper

Instructions

①Refer to Lesson 10; make two sets by joining five spirals onto the left and the right. Cut the stitches from 7.5 cm (3") of each of the donut cuts and join together. Two pieces can be made, for the front and the back.

②Refer to the diagram and attach the solid brown cloth, the quilt cotton and backing on top, and quilt.

③Make two 4 cm × 40 cm (1 1/2" × 16") solid brown handles.

④Cut the lining the same size as in step ②.

⑤Sew two 50 cm × 65 cm (19 1/2" × 25 1/2") pieces of solid brown cloth onto the sides of the zipper. Turn the lining back to front and tack the zipper in place.

⑥Sew the cloth with zipper attached into the opening from step ②.   At this time, place the 40 cm (16") handles on and sew into place.

⑦Make the bag from the front of step 2 and sew the gusset.

⑧Sew the back of step 4 in the same way. Put this into the front of the bag, and finish the lining. (There is a pocket in the lining as shown in the diagram)

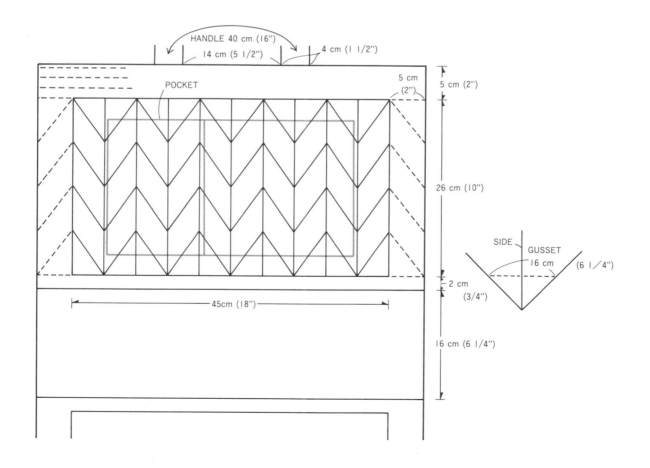

POCHET (LESSON 10) FROM PAGE 60

Finished size bag width 26 cm (10") depth 22 cm (8 1/2")

Materials

Cloth for bajero (printed and plain) 4.5 cm × 110 cm (1 3/4" × 43"); several types

backing cloth and lining; adequate amounts of each.

Quilt cotton 25 cm (10") square 22 cm (8 1/2") zipper Small amount of yarn 1 cm (3/8") wide leather shoulder strap

Instructions

①Refer to Lesson 10; Bajero and make front side.

②Insert the bajero design as in the diagram, attach the bottom cloth, and quilt.

③Cut the lining the same size as in step ②.

④Sew the sides together with piping holding yarn.

⑤Sew the lining the same as the front and insert it into the front bag.

⑥Sew the double bias tape unto the opening formed by matching up the front and lining. (4 cm (1 1/2") wide bias is folded in the middle) At this time hook the clips onto each side of the bag, place the folded bias tape onto the inside of the opening and sew the zipper onto this.

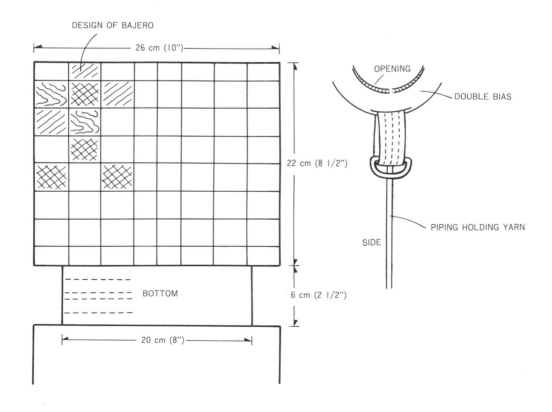

SMALL BAG (LESSON 10) FROM PAGE 60

Finished size   bag width 23 cm (9") depth 20 cm (8")
Materials
Cloth A (remnants from spiral design, etc.); cloth B (bag cloth) adequate
amounts of each. Cord (fine cotton braid) 120 cm (47")
Instructions
①Attach preferred side of cloth B onto the left and right side of cloth A. If
you would like a diagonal design attach the cloth diagonally.
②After sewing cord slot, fold in half and make the bag. (Pinch the width of
the gusset and sew between the seams on the sides.)
③Pass the cord through the sides in turn, as in the diagram, and tie.

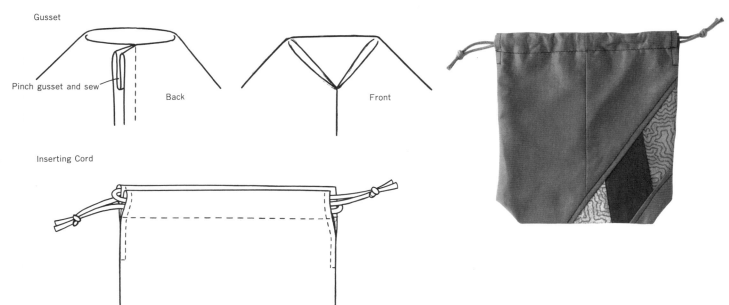

Gusset

Pinch gusset and sew

Back

Front

Inserting Cord

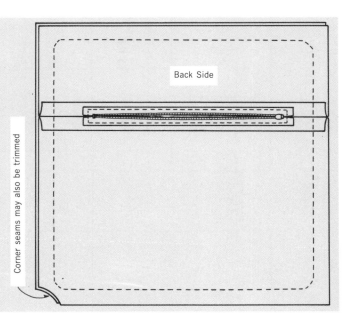

ASSEMBLING   THE

Leave the back side of the zipper open (Refer to
page 69). Turn front side and back side inside
out and sew hem. Sew the corners round. Turn
over. Insert the cushion straighten out and
finish.

Corner seams may also be trimmed

Back Side

LINGERIE CASE (LESSON 10) FROM PAGE 60

Finished size 22 cm × 29 cm (8 1/2" × 11 1/2")

Materials

Cloth A (five kinds for bajero), Cloth B (main section, piping), liner backing; 29 cm x 56 cm (11 1/2" × 22"), One 2.5 cm (1") wood button

Instructions

①Make bajero design from cloth A. (five 4.5 cm (1 3/4") strips) (Refer to Bajero in Lesson 10)

②Sew cloth B to step ①. (Refer to diagram)

③Cut the lining the same size as in step ②, and attach the pocket. (Refer to the diagram)

④Make 2 meters of 3.5 cm (1 1/4") · wide bias tape from cloth B. (Refer to page 67)

⑤Insert backing between steps ② and ③, and wrap bias from step 4 around this. (Insert the button loop into the bias as in the diagram) Sew on the button.

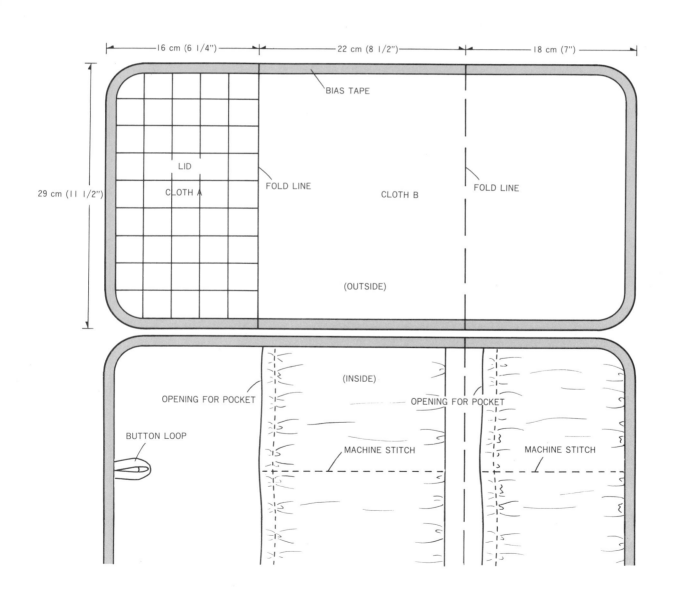

COSMETICS POUCH (LESSON 10)

FROM PAGE 61

[Large Cosmetics Pouch]

Finished size 17 cm × 26 cm (7" × 10")

Materials

Three types 4.5 cm × 110 cm (1 3/4" × 43") for Seminole band, adequate amounts of Accent Cloth, Cloth for main section, and Lining.

Quilt cotton; adequate amount, 30 cm (12") zipper

Instructions

①Refer to Seminole in Lesson 10 and make Seminole band.

②Sew Seminole, accent cloth, and main section together from center as seen in the diagram.

③Place lining and quilt cloth on step ② and quilt as shown in the diagram. (Quilting may be done diagonally)

④Cut 3.5 cm (1 1/2") wide bias from the same cloth as used in main section. (Surroundings)

⑤From the front side, sew around the bias of step 4 onto step 3. Iron the bias back and blind stitch to the binding.

⑥Fold step 5 in half attach zipper onto the protruding side.

⑦The bias should be sewn back with fine stitching at the sides. Pinch a 4 cm (1 1/2") gusset and sew.

⑧Sew the zipper onto the inside and finish.

[Small Cosmetics Pouch]

Finished size 15 cm × 15 cm (6" × 6")

Materials

Three types for Seminole, Main section cloth, and Lining; adequate amounts of each

Quilt cotton; adequate amount, 20 cm (8") zipper

Instructions

①Sew together as in the diagram, cut at 3.5 cm (1 1/2").

②Offset and piece as in the diagram. Width of Seminole band is 4.5 cm (1 3/4).

③Make as shown in diagram. Assembly is same as for large pouch.

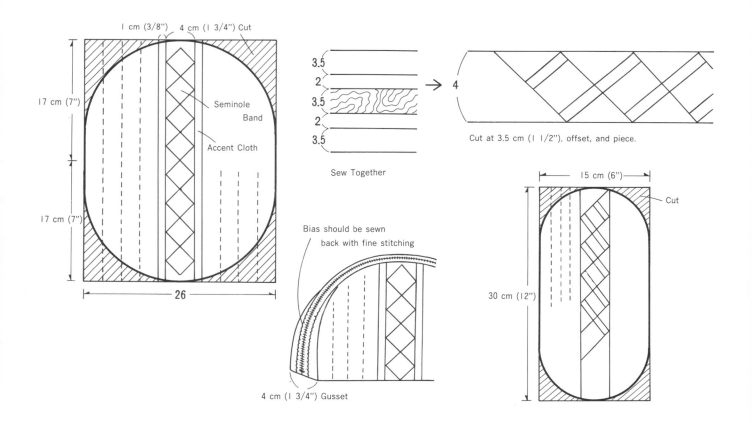

SMALL BAG (LESSON 11)

FROM PAGE 64

Finished size   20 cm × 20 cm (8" × 8")

Materials

Cloth A (five types of cloth for rose), Cloth B (main section),and Lining (black); sufficient amounts of each, 2 m (79") narrow black satin cord

Instructions

①Make the rose block from cloth A. (Refer to paper piecing in Lesson 9)

②Attach cloth B around the edges of cloth from step ①.   (Refer to diagram, make the back the same size and join the pieces at the bottom)

③Cut lining the same size as step ②.

④Assembling the small bag: Turn front cloth step ② inside-out and fold in half to the middle of the bottom. Fold lining from step 3 the same way. Place the two cloths together and sew from the bottom to halfway up the sides. Sew the remaining front cloth and lining separately to 5 cm (2") from the top. (Refer to the diagram) Turn over and the lining is attached. Sew a 3 cm (1 1/4") gusset.   Fold remaining 5 cm (2") (cord slot) into 0.5 cm (1/4") and machine stitch. Fold opening to 0.5 cm (1/4") and machine stitch. (Forms the cord slot)

⑤Pass cord through both sides. (Refer to page 90)

ROSE BLOCK (ACTUAL SIZE PATTERN)

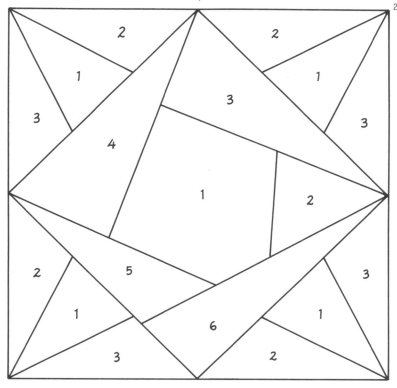

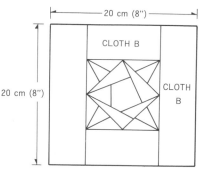

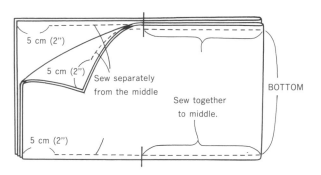

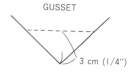

VEST (LESSON 11) FROM PAGE 64

[Black]

Finished size One size fits all

Materials

Cloth A (main section cloth), Cloth B (two types for Seminole) adequate amount of Lining, 4 cm (1 1/2") wide Tyrolean tape 60 cm (23 1/2"), Quilt cotton (flannel or sheeting may be used instead)

Instructions

①Make Seminole band from cloth B. (Refer to Lesson 7; Seminole)

②Cut quilt cotton a bit larger than the pattern (about 5 cm larger than the edge). (Actual pattern is on pages 97-99) Refer to Lesson 11; Pressed Quilt and insert evenly cloth A, Seminole band, Seminoles I, and II, and Tyrolean tape, and piece. (Refer to the diagram) Make the right and left sides of the front of the main body.

③Place pattern onto step ② and cut the pattern. Cut the back of the body the same way as the cloth A and the quilt cotton.

④Place the quilt cotton and cloth A and sew the on the Seminole band to imitate a belt. (Seminole I)

⑤Cut the lining the same size as in step ③.

⑥Assemble into a vest. (Refer to page 96)

SEMINOLE I

4.5 cm × 110 cm
(1 3/4" × 43")

5 cm × 110 cm
(2" × 43")

4.5 cm × 110 cm
(1 3/4" × 43")

SEMINOLE I

10 cm (4")

SEMINOLE II

5 cm × 110 cm
(2" × 43")

5 cm × 110 cm
(2" × 43")

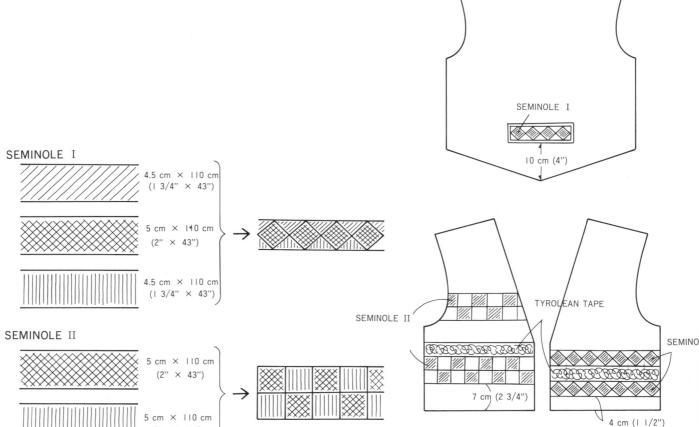

SEMINOLE II

TYROLEAN TAPE

SEMINO

7 cm (2 3/4")

4 cm (1 1/2")

[Pink]

Finished size One size fits all

Materials

Cloth A (main section cloth), Cloth B (four types for Seminole band), Lining; adequate amount 3.8 cm (1 1/2") wide Tyrolean tape 50 cm (19 3/4"), Quilt cotton (flannel or sheeting may be used instead)

Instructions

①Make the Seminole band from cloth B.
②Make three knots from cloth A (use Fabric Manipulation), as in the diagram.
③Make Prairie Points (use Fabric Manipulation), as in the diagram.
④finished designs from steps ① to ③ Insert the Tyrolean tape as shown in the photo and make the right and left sides of the front body using the pressed quilt method. (Vest assembly is same as in black vest, refer to page 96)

②Make Knot

3 cm × 12 cm

Fold in half and sew (0.5 cm (3/16") seam)   Turn back around and tie at the center Make three

③Make Prairie Point

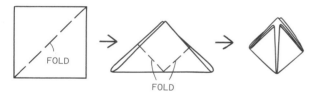

FOLD   FOLD

SEMINOLE I

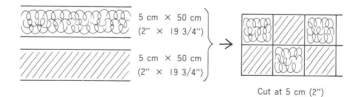

5 cm × 50 cm (2" × 19 3/4")

5 cm × 50 cm (2" × 19 3/4")

Cut at 5 cm (2")

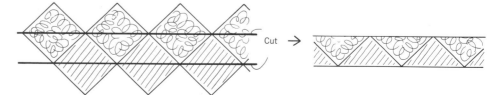

Cut →

※Offset and join pieces together

● ASSEMBLING THE VEST

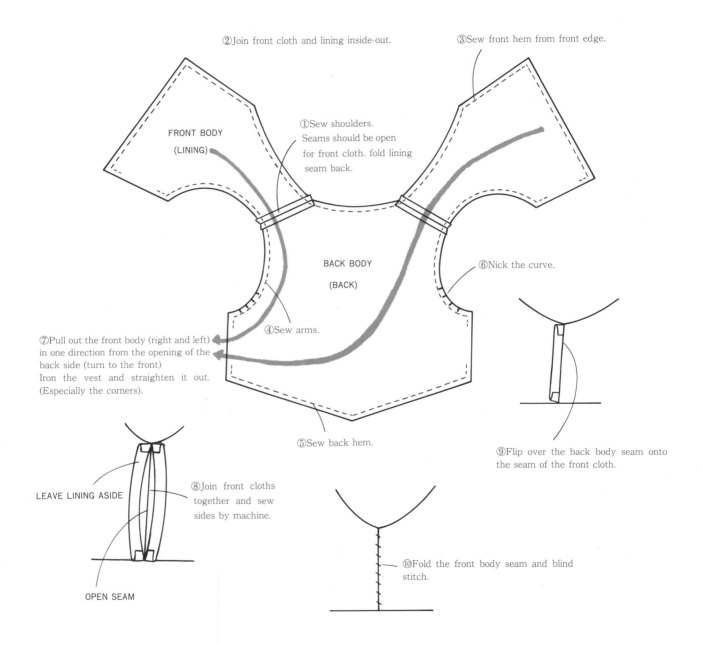

②Join front cloth and lining inside-out.

③Sew front hem from front edge.

FRONT BODY

(LINING)

①Sew shoulders.
Seams should be open
for front cloth. fold lining
seam back.

BACK BODY

(BACK)

⑥Nick the curve.

⑦Pull out the front body (right and left)
in one direction from the opening of the
back side (turn to the front)
Iron the vest and straighten it out.
(Especially the corners).

④Sew arms.

⑤Sew back hem.

⑨Flip over the back body seam onto
the seam of the front cloth.

LEAVE LINING ASIDE

⑧Join front cloths
together and sew
sides by machine.

OPEN SEAM

⑩Fold the front body seam and blind
stitch.

※It is better to use soft quilt cotton in making such
clothing as vests or jackets. Flannel or sheeting may
be used. If the clothing is to be made thin, use only the
lining.